At the Cross
With Mary

At the Cross
With Mary

The Life and Message of
Saint Gabriel of the Sorrowful Virgin.

By
John Joseph D. Schweska, K.H.S.

MANCIPIA PRESS
Saint Benedict Center • Still River • Massachusetts • 01467
www.saintbenedict.com

Produced and designed by Mancipia Studios
The Slaves of the Immaculate Heart of Mary,
Saint Benedict Center, Still River, MA. 01467
www.saintbenedict.com

ISBN: 0-9716822-3-2

Many images used with permission from The ECO Press;
"Boy in a Hurry" by Camillus Barth C.P.

Table of Contents

Dedication

I gratefully dedicate this new edition of the life and study of Saint Gabriel to Our Lady of Lourdes in honor of the 150th Jubilee of Apparitions to Saint Bernadette, 1858-2008, remembering Mary's call to the world for a deeper life of Eucharistic union, prayer, penance, and charity—lived in the light of her Son's Holy Cross.

Introduction

The Story of Saint Gabriel Possenti

Boy of Compassion

Blessed Pope John XXIII had a special devotion to Saint Gabriel. The Holy Father, always immersed in the Precious Blood mystery and devotion since he was a young boy, wrote in a Letter (1962) in observance of the Centenary of Saint Gabriel's death, that we should "behold" and "study" Saint Gabriel, a mirror of prayer and holiness—a sanctity found at the Cross and in the Blood of Jesus, always with Mary as our companion and spiritual tutor, as she was Gabriel's.

Saint Gabriel was born in Assisi, Italy, on March 1, 1838, of Agnes and Sante Possenti, in the living quarters of the governor's palace. The child's father, Sante Possenti, was an illustrious political figure in the Vatican State and was appointed governor of Assisi in 1837. The family also consisted of Lawrence, Paul, Maria Luisa, Teresa, Louis, Michael, Henry, and Adele. (Two other children, Louis and Paul, had died at the age of three, one in 1827 and another in the following year.) The prosperous family had experienced intense loss and pain over these deaths. Agnes was soon to give birth again in 1839 to Vincent and in 1840 to Rosa.

The future saint was blessed in being born in a city immortalized by the seraphic saints, Francis and Clare. The child was immediately carried by his parents to the Basilica of Saint Ruffino where he was baptized in the ancient font. The tiny infant was christened Francis in honor of the city's great saint and father, and the added names of Joseph Vincent Pacifico Rufino were attached to it. His family simply called him Francis or by his nickname, Checchino, and sometimes, just "Chino." For the first three years and eight months of his life, he was nurtured in the holy atmosphere of Assisi; he developed a great devotion to Saint Francis for the rest of his life, and like him, a call to affinity with the poor and suffering, to Christ's Passion, to Mary as mother, in a spirit of penance and with genuine joy.

In October, 1841, Francis's father was chosen as the Grand Judge or Assessor of Spoleto, an important, cultural city. The family transferred to their new home, a large rented flat in an impressive building–situated in the heart of the twisting streets and cobbled stairways of town. Soon after, Rosa died; she was seven months old. In quick succession, Adele died at the age of nine, of diphtheria. The mother was grief stricken, causing her already delicate health to decline. Suddenly, meningitis attacked her. Four-year-old Francis had grown extremely attached to his mother, loving to listen to her stories of the saints, and receiving the benefits of her loving attention.

Now, with all his siblings, he was called to her deathbed. Like Saint Therese of Lisieux, who also lost her mother at the same tender age as Francis, he never forgot the impressive moment of his mother's death. Agne's Fransciscan confessor and the family prayed with her before her final departure from this life, and in their midst she peacefully died. Francis, realizing Agnes would never speak to him again or hold him, ran throughout the entire apartment loudly crying out, "My Mama!" The child was inconsolable for some time until he allowed his 13-year-old sister, Maria Louisa, to comfort him. Later, a governess named Pacifica, whom Francis grew very fond of, did her best to fill his mother's former role. Nonetheless, Francis felt orphaned. It was here, in the first striking experience of emptiness and deprivation in his life, that perhaps God found space to mother and father the boy, establishing a real relationship with him.

Maria Luisa, a pious and mature girl for her age, continued the catechetical lessons to her siblings that her mother had been so faithful in doing. During these periods of instruction, she noticed that the Blessed

Mother had an early attraction for her little brother, Francis, and in the Virgin's maternal-looking statues and paintings, the boy seemed to easily identify with the tenderness and care which his earthly mother impressed upon him. It seems that the Holy Spirit began to create gentle stirrings at this time in the future saint's wounded heart. This boy, later as a youth and a young man, would always understand the pain of losing a loved one and exhibited a keen sense of compassion for others, especially the poor and abandoned. (Gabriel is indeed their advocate, as well as for all who work to aid the less fortunate!) Already, the child had attached himself to a little image of the Pieta, the Sorrowful Mother of Jesus. Empathizing with the loss of Mary's son, expressed in the form of the art piece, the child wanted so much to try to console the Mother of God. Kneeling before the statue with a votive light his sister had placed there, Francis began to pray very naturally by speaking about his feelings and sharing with the Lady the little episodes of his boyhood. He never forgot this statue where his prayer life began. Years later, as a seminarian, he was to write home to his father: " ...In closing, I recall to you the statue of the Pieta. Honor her as much as you can, and do not doubt that you will experience her benign assistance." (Farnum, *Saint Gabriel*, p. 116).

Youth of Indecision

In 1844, Francis was admitted to the fine instructions of the School of the Christian Brothers and they prepared him well to receive the sacraments of Confirmation in 1846, and First Holy Communion in 1850. During this time, Francis enjoyed all the comforts of a prosperous family but he had an unusual penchant for the poor and suffering and was often scolded for giving away huge amounts of food from the family kitchen when beggars came to the servants' door for alms. His own childhood suffering taught him to feel for the wounded. This empathy, in turn, stretched even wider his naturally generous heart. His brother Michael expressed admiration for a gold watch and chain which Francis had recently received as a gift. Almost immediately, Francis took the watch off and gave it to his brother, saying, "I want you to have it!" This scene characterizes the entire spiritual life that was the boy's and the donation of himself to Christ and the service of the Church that he would one day make.

However, he was far from being a born saint! He was known for a quick temper, and a certain irascibility. Having a dispute with one of his brothers, he ran after the boy who, being hotly pursued, slammed a door into Francis' nose! This caused a slight bump on the ridge of his fine aquiline nose, the butt of good-humored jokes by his friends. Despite his faults, his affectionate nature and willingness to quickly ask forgiveness of those he offended won everyone's hearts. With the guidance of Maria Luisa and the governess, the boy slowly tried to amend whatever negative traits he had manifested.

Maria Pannechetti, a daughter of Sante Possenti's friends, was developing a special relationship with Francis. Many expected them to marry. Philip Giovannetti was his best friend and they shared mutual

love for school, sports, and an interest in religion. Francis' life appeared easy, simple and full of peace. But a turbulent split in his mind existed that he could not quite integrate within himself. There was an undulating desire to give himself completely to God, a God of love, and a God who had become flesh and was crucified out of love for him. Very much like the vocation story of Francis of Assisi, the modern Francis grappled with the call of God; people noticed that the once happy-go-lucky Francis was stealing time away in various churches and in the hills to hide himself in prayer.

His writings, poems and compositions at college began to reflect a theological insight into the poverty of God's emptying Himself out for humankind. Three times Francis had made secret promises to become a religious (once even formally applying to the Jesuits for admission to their novitiate); each time was at some moment of crisis: a fever he experienced, a near-fatal hunting accident (when he fell from a horse and his rifle exploded–the bullet just missing his face), and later, a throat infection that almost killed him. Francis, always quickly recovering, soon forgot about the promises and told the Jesuit spiritual director that he was not sure about his vocation. He was obviously torn between the tremendous vista of opportunities that his innate gifts, coupled with what his family connections afforded him–and his intense spiritual experiences which beckoned him to some greater mission he could not yet define.

A British Passionist, who after having had the opportunity to interview Francis' still surviving brother, Dr. Michael Possenti, in 1930, perceived "that Saint Gabriel, (the former Francis Possenti) who understands the torments of indecision from his own prolonged personal experience, will have special sympathy and understanding for those who are similarly tormented." (*Gabriel Possenti: Student, Passionist, Saint: Interview with Dr. Michael Possenti,* p.4)

Saint Gabriel, a patron of the poor and afflicted, is also a compassion-

4

ate counselor to the undecided. As a guide for youth and young adults, he empathizes with their search for deeper meaning and a desire to do something worthwhile with their lives. He can also help middle-aged and even elderly adults who today, more than ever before, are risking career changes in order to seek more creative and fuller lives. Many people come to realize that they initially pursued certain goals because of the expectations of others; fortunately, with grace, they finally listen to God's inner call within them and the mission they must fulfill. Saint Gabriel, who had to struggle to accomplish his own personal dream, is there for them as a friend and inspiration.

Called by Mary!

In 1848, a number of city revolts led eventually to a national movement for the unification of Italy and the termination of the large Papal territories. Sante Possenti, an employee of the Vatican State for his entire law career, was placed under extreme pressure. The political situation involved religious sentiments and confused loyalties, even in the Possenti household. A series of losses were to contribute to and shape the direction of Gabriel's future vocation. Paul Possenti died when he was 21 years old in the military hospital at Chioggia. He had enlisted to defend the papal lands but soon died of food poisoning. In 1853, tragedy struck the family again. Lawrence, a former seminarian and a short-term medical student, and eventually an engineer by profession, committed suicide in a rented apartment in Rome. According to later testimony by his sister, Teresa, the family always maintained "much reserve' about this issue. The circulating rumor that Lawrence was heart-broken over some romance was false. The suicide was connected with Lawrence's association with Freemasonry and he was reportedly involved with a commission to murder a man. Teresa thought that her brother preferred suicide to murder. She said that Francis was not told right away about his brother's death because of his sensitivity. The details were slowly revealed to him as time passed. (Cavatassi & Giorgini, *Fonti,* p.255)

Finally, Francis' sister, Maria Luisa, a second mother to him, fell victim to cholera in 1855. The pain of this loss was indescribable for Francis and the family. In particular, for Francis, the realization of the shortness and unpredictability of life itself began to be the source of his thoughts. He again returned to the idea of religious life. His father, Sante, however, had great secular plans for his favorite son. He did everything he could to distract his son from grief and melancholy and any further ideas of the cloister.

Sante insisted that Francis frequent the theatre again and attend more dances. But by the following year, in the summer of 1856, the father's plans were totally foiled. It seemed that the Blessed Mother herself intervened and called her spiritual son, Francis, to the religious life. While the Byzantine Icon of Mary was carried in procession through the streets of Spoleto on August 22, 1856, Francis heard Mary's voice in the depths of his heart: "Francis, what are you doing in the world? You were not made for the world. Follow your vocation!" (Battistelli, *S. Gabriele Dell'Addolorata,* p.52) Francis would never forget this

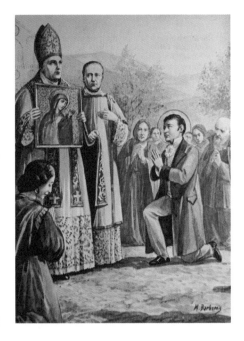

grace, nor ever doubt its reality. It was the end to all indecision. It was the birth of a new man and a new life. Once he had felt a division in him, but now he experienced freedom and wholeness.

Mary, who had captured Gabriel's heart since he was a toddler, was now calling him into a final determination and grace to follow God's plan for him as a religious. It is amazing how totally Gabriel gave himself over to Mary's reign through his love and devotion, and in the exercise of every act of charity and sacrifice he would henceforth render in her honor. It was Mary who was to bring Gabriel into the depths of Calvary to be immersed in the Crucified Lord's love, glory, and as Saint Paul the Apostle writes, "the folly" of the Cross—the very "Wisdom of God"! The holy Cardinal Parocchi, in his letter to Pope Leo XIII, wrote: " Mary was the very soul of Gabriel's life, the source and model of the sanctity to which he attained; so that it may be truly said, that in his devotion to the great Mother of God, he has scarcely been equaled by any even of the greatest saints….that this holy youth had been raised up in the Church by God, to serve as a model of filial love and reverence to all the clients of the most holy Virgin." (Hage, p. 207) Amazing and beautiful are the words of Pope Leo XIII about Gabriel: "Because of his filial love for Mary at the foot of the Cross, he deserves to take his place by the side of Saint John, the beloved disciple to whom Christ in His dying hour commended His

Mother." Fittingly then, the title of this book's new edition is named *By the Cross with Mary*.

Man of Determination

Francis quickly obeyed the Lady of the icon's suggestion! He commenced an application process and obtained the necessary documents needed to be sent to the religious order of his choice–the Passionists, founded by Paul of the Cross in 1720. This congregation observed an ascetic rule in memory of the Passion of the Lord. Their charism was quite unique: the founder's followers were to be zealous missionaries and preachers of "the Word of the Cross," renewing the faithful in their faith and love for God; afterwards, the missioners were to return to a "retreat" (the name used to describe the function and meaning of their monasteries) and replenish their spiritual lives in a penitential, and deeply prayerful life. Although the Passionists are not truly canonical "monks," they originally assumed the title for themselves because of the monastic lifestyle that developed in their retreats. The characteristics of this life were (and still are) penance, prayer, solitude, and poverty. The two-sided aspects of "missioner-monk" of the Passionist vocation were ideal for Francis Possenti; it promised a place for the hermit within him, and an outlet for the talented orator and scholar he was.

Why did Francis choose the Passionists, one of the most rigorous rules of religious life at that time? He had been under the strong influence of the Jesuits and had once shown great interest in them. Why didn't he join the Dominicans, the order of preachers, with whom his brother, Louis, was already a professed friar? Many have pondered why Francis did not become a Franciscan; after all, he was always devoted to his namesake, the seraphic Francis of Assisi. Why was he not compelled to live the Franciscan penitential rule? He was also well aware of his kind and inspiring uncle, Father John Baptist, who belonged to the strict observance of the Capuchins. However, Francis chose a congregation that was unfamiliar to his background and environment. How did this come about? It is most likely that Paul of the Cross and his congregation must have been discussed and read about in Francis' academic circle. The founder had been recently beatified in 1853, a notorious event in the Papal States. Impressive literature was most definitely distributed to religious groups and schools; in fact two other Jesuit students, Caesar Calandrelli and Ponziano Gusmondi, were joining the Passionists. Without question, Francis spoke with them about their daring decision. The immense sacrifice of self which the Passionist rule demanded, as well as the novelty of the order, was undoubtedly a great attraction and challenge for so idealistic a youth as Francis. He had lived in luxury and prestige like the young man in John's Gospel; now he was ready to forsake everything and completely follow the "poor Jesus," intimately embracing the "Lord's Cross" and "Sorrowful Mother"–striking images for the Passionist, as well as Francis' own childhood spirituality.

Francis never received a letter of reply from the Passionist provincial, not because it was not sent, but because Francis' father, Sante, had intercepted the post and kept the letter of acceptance from his son. He obviously was not in approval of this far-away congregation and its strict life. Sante was probably convinced that this was another passing fancy for Francis. The judge argued, and would ever after continue to argue that his son's health had always been too "delicate" for the rigors and fastings of monastic life. A brilliant career in law awaited the youth–if only he accepted the opportunity! And if he must be a priest, thought Sante, why not the Jesuits or the diocese which offered so much more opportunity in different areas of advancement to a bright young man?

Francis wrote a second letter to the provincial; there was still no answer. He decided to depart for the Passionist novitiate in Morravale without any assurance of acceptance. It would be a journey of faith. However, before the departure, Francis would fulfill his last societal obligation in the Spoletan limelight as main orator for the closing of the academic year–the Jesuit Awards Night. He wore his finest clothing and gave a compelling speech. Several academic medals were awarded to him that night. Many dignitaries and family friends extended congratulations to Francis. All eyes were on him, including Maria Pannechetti's. Everyone wondered what university Francis would attend, what profession he had chosen.

Judge Possenti must have been heart-broken as he alone knew his son's secret plans for leaving on the morrow, abandoning all the dreams others had for him! More than ever before, Francis' bright future in the world seemed powerfully real; the next day they would be but a father's lost dream. Unfortunately, Sante always seemed locked in his own ambitions for his son. The festive celebrations followed with music, food, and expressive, vivid conversation. The affair was too loud and too filled with glitter for Francis. He had to get away and be quiet with someone he trusted. He sought out his friend, Philip, and asked him to go out for a while and enjoy the night air. They walked up and down the stone laden streets of Spoleto, reveling in their comfortable friendship. Francis quietly observed the familiar and historical sites of the city, and pondered poignantly that this was to be his last night in the world as he had known it. He said nothing of his plans to Philip for fear of Philip's resistance to a Passionist vocation; the night was too beautiful to spoil. When Francis returned to his room, he sat down at the desk and wrote a long letter to Philip, and to Maria and her family regarding his call to the Passionists and the journey he was about to take. He bid them farewell and promised them his loving prayers.

At dawn, on September 6, 1856, his journey to the Passionists began, a journey of sheer determination against much family opposition. In a highly pressurized Italian family network, this was no easy accomplishment. In going against a strong-willed father and successful diplomat who wanted the very best for his family and its reputation and prosperity, Francis indeed appeared to be a new young man who finally knew what he wanted and would have it at all costs. A unique individualism set him on an unknown path to face an unsure future–but with a confidence that he was guided and upheld by God. This sense of new, unbounded security disarmed his father and all who tried to convince him that the Passionists were really not for him. It was not long before the Spoletans at home were buzzing with the news... "The dancer?! To the Passionists?...He'll be back soon enough!" They were wrong.

Francis Becomes "Confrater Gabriel"

On September 9, Francis arrived at the Retreat of Our Lady of the Oak. The Passionists had not given up hope for his arrival; they had suspected a possible problem with the postal system. The other postulants arrived earlier, but Francis was able to catch up with their program. On September 21, Francis received the coarse black habit of penance. Sandals replaced his customary shoes. He was reminded by the director that he was stripping himself of the old person and putting on a new self. (Col. 3:10) To further signify this, he was called by a new name: Confrater Gabriel of the Sorrowful Virgin. (Confrater was a traditional title used at one time to address a religious brother studying for priesthood in contrast to the "fraters" who wished to remain lay brothers.)

Saint Gabriel the Archangel, who announced the message of the Incarnation, became Francis' new patron; like him, Francis Possenti was to announce Good News. The religious title "of the Sorrowful Virgin," added in place of his family name, truly confirmed his boyhood love and devotion to the Pieta. Forever after this, the Church and the world would know Francis by the name *Gabriel*, and by the Lady he cherished. Father Raphael was the kind and able novice master, but it was another priest, nine years older than Gabriel, Father Norbert Cassinelli of Saint Mary,

(now proclaimed "Venerable") who would make all the difference in this student's life. Father Norbert was to become an intimate companion and spiritual director to the future saint. The individualism that propelled Gabriel to follow his personal call now gave way to an enthusiastic obedience which would allow Norbert to guide him. Gabriel's openness and purity of intention predisposed him to reveal his inner soul and its movements to his director. Gabriel wanted everything rooted out that would weaken his resolve to surrender everything to God's love. He readily told Norbert: "Everything in me must go that is not for God!" (Poage, *Son of the Passion,* p.102) For almost six and a half years, Norbert and Gabriel were to share a rare gift of spiritual union. This union developed into a unique spiritual friendship that would transcend human boundaries. It is more than likely that without Father Norbert, Gabriel would not have become the saint he is.

Likewise, Norbert's life was sanctified and renewed in his appreciation for all things Passionist and Marian by his participation in Gabriel's pure joy and enthusiasm for Christ and his mother. The teacher was training the student, while the future saint was enlivening the vocation of his mentor. Today, Gabriel remains a true companion to religious, priests, and seminarians who are praying for a renewal or deepening of their spiritual lives and for the efficacy of their ministries. Interestingly, although Gabriel was never ordained a priest, Blessed Pope John XXIII made a special point to advise those called to be priests to look at Saint Gabriel's love for prayer and try to imitate his "life of intense spirituality" in their busy ministries. (*Passionist Archives,* Rome)

On September 22, 1857, Confrater Gabriel made his perpetual vows as a Passionist–poverty, chastity and obedience, as well as a unique fourth vow attached to all Passionists' professions–to promote devotion to the

Passion of the Lord. The striking, white-edged and heart-shaped badge of a Passionist, representing Jesus' sufferings and bearing his Name, was attached to Gabriel's habit over his heart. (This sign is believed to have been received in two interior visions by the founder; in one apparition, the Blessed Virgin herself presented the badge of the Passion of Jesus.) Now, Gabriel wore this mystical sign. The first and greatest part of his dream was fulfilled–to be a true religious–what his very core of self called out for him to be. But there was still something else. He would now begin studies for what he believed was the other, vital part of his vocation–to be a priest of Jesus Christ!

Brother of the Beatitudes

As a Passionist student, Gabriel followed a required horarium–a schedule of set times–for meditation, study, classes, chanting of the Divine Office, meals, and recreation. Gabriel achieved remarkable advancement in the ways of an obedient and cheerful religious. He excelled in every simple task; each ordinary work or act became a gift in return to God. If the famed Therese of Lisieux is to compared with a male counterpart in her 'little way" of confidence in God and in doing the ordinary things extraordinarily well, then Gabriel surely is her soul mate! Father Norbert would remark years later at Gabriel's beatification ceremony in 1908, "... what he did, he did with all his heart!" *(Burke, Happy Was My Youth, p.7)* Saint Paul's first epistle to the Corinthians expresses this spirit well: *Your every act should be done with love. (16:4)*

In the monotony of the same, daily scheme of things, Gabriel found a quiet framework to develop the resources of his inner life, time to tackle the truth of who he was and to refine it by cooperating with the Spirit at work in him. The workings of his soul became more and more evident to those around him. They saw that he had a knack for calming others and being a peacemaker. His love for the poor and suffering was expressed by managing to set aside portions of his own meals for the poor in the area. Again, Blessed John XXIII speaks of Gabriel's life and spirit as remarkably "akin to Saint Francis of Assisi and his love for Lady Poverty." (*Passionist Archives,* Rome)

A compassionate nature gave Gabriel a ministerial bent; Father Norbert keenly observed this and gave his charge permission to reach out to persons who might be in need. As the students took their recreational walks in the countryside, Gabriel was able to touch the lives of the people, and they remembered these encounters with him–talks of prayer and religious education or moments of encouragement and compassion. Fellow students were also recipients of his generosity. He was living the beatitudes of Christ, simply but powerfully.

Gabriel's unusual charm, coupled with sincere faith, inspired the country folk who heard him during the students' "ferverinos" (little sermons or stories to stir one's heart to fervor for God) at the devotional services in the chapel. He was genuine, and it seemed to them that he believed what he was preaching! The Passionists' neighbors recognized Gabriel as a holy man in their midst. Through his interest and concern for them, he was a living sign of God's own constant love and presence among them.

Gabriel spent another year at Morravale studying philosophy. Further philosophy studies were continued at the Retreat of Saint Augustine in Pievetorina. The class, as well as Father Norbert, was transferred there on June 20, 1858. The marshes of this area proved to be an unhealthy atmosphere and aggravated the already existing respiratory problems from which Gabriel had often suffered. In August, the much loved family governess of fourteen years, Pacifica Cucci, came to visit her favorite former charge. Gabriel was excited to see her but resisted the message she brought from his father that there would be no shame in leaving the Passionists if his health did not allow him to live their rule of life. Pacifica argued that he should, at least, think about a period of convalescence in the comforts of his Spoletan home. Gabriel treated Pacifica with loving respect and concern but told her his answer in no uncertain terms. She reported back to the judge that his son's response was "No!" and "Never!" The following month, Judge Possenti sent Gabriel's brother, Michael, a medical student, to convince Gabriel of the same thing that Pacifica had already failed to do. Michael was also defeated, although deeply moved by his brother's convictions.

A year later, the war for Italy's unity intensified and the dangers of guerilla warfare and bandits became a real threat to the students, the future hope of the Passionist Congregation. On July 4, 1859, the students and staff for theological studies were transferred for safety to the Passionists' most remote Retreat at the highest plateau of the Apennines, under the snow-capped peak, "the Gran Sasso," (The Great Rock), nearly 10,000 feet above sea level. The town, Isola del Gran Sasso (Island of the Great Rock) was so named because it was surrounded by two mountain rivers that converged. The monks arrived to this magnificent sight on July 10. During Gabriel's two and a half years at this location, he would firmly establish himself in the hearts of the mountain people, of the Abruzzi region; in fact, John XXIII would later proclaim him their special patron.

It was not long before clear signs of serious illness began to set in, fits of coughing and acute respiratory distress. Norbert called in the local doctors and they tried to assist Gabriel with the limited remedies of the time. On May 25, 1861, Gabriel was well enough to go with his class to the Cathedral in Penne to receive minor orders, the first rites toward priesthood. Norbert wrote to Sante Possenti that he was sure that his son's health would improve and that the excellent air of the mountains would benefit him. He added that if conditions were safe and all went well that he was confident that Gabriel would sing his first Mass by Christmas Day of that year. (Burke, p. 202). But the political situation worsened and traveling became impossible. Ordination to sub-deacon, planned for September, was cancelled.

Around November, the young man suffered his first attack of hemoptysis, the coughing up of blood, and was diagnosed with bronchial tuberculosis. In Gabriel's day, this illness was terminal. Not only was his hope for the priesthood–which he could almost touch now–dashed, but his very young life, full of promise and vitality, were seemingly being robbed from him.

Gabriel managed to turn the disappointment into a final gift to his Creator. He believed that God's Will was evident in this sequence of events and recognized an opportunity to share in the true emotions and physical pain of Jesus' Passion. Very importantly, Gabriel saw this disease as a doorway to heaven and total unity with God. He truly believed that this was the great adventure for him! Gabriel, who often quoted scripture in his letters home, and had avidly studied the Word of God, now became a living testimony to it by his manner of living and attitude in dying:

But the things that were gain to me, the same I have counted loss for Christ. Furthermore, I count all things to be but loss for the excellent knowledge of Jesus Christ my Lord; for whom I have suffered the loss of all things, and count them but as dung, that I may gain Christ...That I may know Him and the power of His Resurrection, and the fellowship of His sufferings, being made conformable to His death, if by any means I may attain to the resurrection which is from the dead. Not as though I had already attained, or were already perfect; but I follow after, if I may by any means apprehend, wherein I am also apprehended by Christ Jesus. Brethren, I do not count myself to have apprehended. But one thing I do: forgetting the things that are behind, and stretching forth myself to those that are before, I press toward the mark, to the prize of the supernal vocation of God in Christ Jesus. (Phil. 3:7-8, 10-14)

Gabriel was becoming a model of hope and courage for all who face death, especially the terminally and chronically ill. Gabriel can also be a

real resource of strength and wisdom for those who deal with the excru-
ciating pain of losing a loved one, and for the caregivers of the dying.
His patience and ongoing kind disposition, even in dying, drew people
near him; fresh milk was delivered by a local farmer for the sick seminarian, and students vied for a space to care for him in the infirmary. Father
Norbert became more than a director–he acted as a faithful friend, praying
with and for Gabriel, always there for him in every need.

Gabriel's illness was a total sharing in the Lord's Passion. In these
final days of physical pain, he also felt tempted to pride; to thwart this
obsession, he had Father Norbert burn his journal of the spiritual life. Ox-
ford scholar and editor, Paul Burns, offers a keen insight upon Gabriel's
decision to destroy the little book, an action "depriving later generations
of a male equivalent of the *Story of a Soul*, as he resembled Saint Therese of Lisieux so closely in his normal childhood, cheerful disposition,
and death from tuberculosis at the age of twenty-four." (Butler's Lives of
the Saints, New Full Edition, February, p. 260) February, 1862, brought
further battles within Gabriel–intense sensual temptations and disturbing thoughts against the Faith. His body contended with physical pain
and complete debilitation. What a marvelous last Communion he had—
trying to kneel on the bed as Father Norbert brought the sacred Viaticum
into the cell. There were continuous prayers and pleas to Our Lady from
Gabriel's lips: "My Mother, make haste!" His devotion to Saint Joseph,
the Angels, and the Holy Souls was evident as he invoked them with great
love and confidence. At last, a period of respite came to him and a final
hour of deep consolation before death. At dawn on February 27, at 6:30
A.M., Gabriel tenderly held a sketch of Christ Crucified and the Sorrowful
Mother. He recited the traditional prayer to Jesus, Mary and Joseph. Before he finished the prayer, he raised himself up, extending his arms in a
welcoming gesture toward the window, his face refulgent and joyful. Then
he sank back and was dead. Norbert glanced around at the others who had
gathered about the bed, and quietly said, "Look...a saint has passed away."
All believed Our Lady had come to escort her son to Heaven. (Wilson, p.12)

Saint of Conversions

Four years later, Victor Emmanuel, the first king of a unified Italy,
suppressed religious congregations; the Passionists were forced to abandon the retreat at Gran Sasso. The Church fell in disrepair but the people
continued to hold the memory of Gabriel. They were acutely aware of his
abandoned tomb and felt his spirit among them. Paul Bonaccia, a college
classmate of Gabriel, wrote his first biography, published in 1868, only

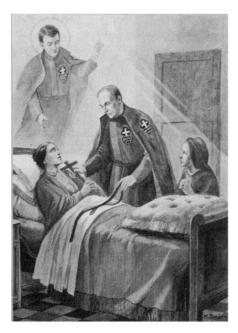

six years after his death. But it was Father Norbert, convinced of Gabriel's remarkable, hidden sanctity, who wrote the story of Gabriel's life that was to be the key testimony; he diligently promoted interest in the youth in his fellow confreres and to the people with whom he engaged.

In 1891, the cause for the beatification was opened. On October 17, 1892, a delegation representing the Passionists and the bishop of Penne arrived at Isola to examine the remains of Confrater Gabriel and to return them to a suitable resting place, a more convenient setting and location. These plans were not advertised and everything was to be done in strict secrecy at that time. However, when the commission approached the old monastery, there were throngs of people coming from every path and road leading up to the plateau of Isola. An estimated number of four thousand appeared in their best of clothing, as if in some grand, formal procession, and this, in spite of it being a work day that required them to be in the fields for the vintage season! Who could explain their presence?

Among them must have been the grown-up children Gabriel taught in the fields and many of the parents who had once heard him speak at the devotions in the chapel. These witnesses must have told others about Gabriel's genuine holiness. His fame spread among them. It also testifies to the Holy Spirit who had wonderfully moved the hearts of these people to assert in a display of love and guardianship that Gabriel had become one of them, that his love for them was real and was being returned, and that they already believed him to be a saint in Heaven, their special intercessor. Mysteriously, indeed, they showed up. Miraculously, for thirty years, Gabriel had spiritually nourished them. They voiced the demand that "their own" saint would not be taken from them, and that nothing was to be done to his remains without their surveillance.

And so the official examination commenced with the appointed laity, one representative from each nearby town. The bones were found in the underground vault; they were reverently gathered and placed in a new tomb in the Church. During this process, a cloud came over the chapel and a heavy downpour of rain was released. The people noticed that it rained nowhere else! Many believed this was a sign of the many graces to came through Gabriel's intercession. By October 23, the first documented cure took place: Father Germanus, (now "Venerable") the official promoter of the cause, placed Gabriel's leather cincture upon Mary Mazzarelli's dying body and encouraged her to invoke the youthful Servant of God. In the morning, Mary instantly recovered and walked down the stairs on her own holding the blessed cincture, and announcing to her stunned family: "Confrater Gabriel has cured me!" Two days later, Mary and her entire family made the "first pilgrimage" of thanksgiving, barefoot, to Gabriel's tomb. A deluge of miracles followed! Father Germanus wrote in 1896: "...the blind see, the dumb speak, the deaf hear, the cripples, the paralytics, and those afflicted with the most serious maladies, some of whom were on their deathbed, have instantaneously recovered their health, by invoking his name." (Hage, p.252)

Although Gabriel has been called "the saint of miracles," it is even more fitting to see him as the *Saint of Conversions* because these miracles were, and are, accompanied with extraordinary spiritual conversions, most often with a desire in the faithful for the sacrament of Penance and the Holy Eucharist. Deeds of charity and hospitality began to flourish among the whole countryside. Soon, people were traveling from distant areas, coming up to the remote and inaccessible mountain town in penitence and prayer.

The Passionists were re-stationed at Gran Sasso to meet the enormous demand for the sacraments. As in his life, Gabriel continued after death to signify that God was tangibly enacting what was stated in Ezekiel: *My tabernacle shall be with them: and I will be their God and they shall be My people.* (37:27) In a strikingly similar way to Saint Therese's mission after death, Gabriel's posthumous mission work was effective, far-reaching, and dramatic–but real, with long-lasting results in the hearts and souls of all who were drawn to him. And like Therese, although non-ordained, he was to participate in and engender a "spiritual" priestly work on earth of offering up everything to God, leading those who invoke him to a revitalization of their relationship with Christ. Those who call upon and walk with Gabriel are challenged by him to do as he did–try to be faithful to the innermost call God gives each individual, wherever, whenever, or in whatever capacity the Lord calls—but always "offering up" our very selves and works as a living act of sacrifice, adoration, atonement, and intercessory love. The most holy and deeply theologically-sound Servant of

God, Pope Pius XII, aptly explained the royal spiritual priesthood of the faithful through sacred Baptism, a true sharing in the Priesthood of Jesus Christ, but he clearly distinguishes at the same time the differences with the ordained priesthood and its very specific privileges and honors given by the laying on of hands passed down to us from the Apostles.

Gabriel had become a living stone in the temple of the Lord! The sanctuary built in his honor in 1914 is now a place for other pilgrims in the faith to become spiritually alive–and like Saint Gabriel, build themselves, with the help of the Holy Spirit, into living sanctuaries for the Presence of God and His love. Saint Gabriel followed the light of Our Lord in the Gospel. The light that Jesus poured into Gabriel and worked through his life could not be hidden or kept under a bushel basket! It was to be placed on a stand–for all to see–so that the Heavenly Father could be praised. (Matt. 5:14-16) Gabriel was beatified on May 31, 1908 by Pope Pius X and canonized a saint in 1920 by Pope Benedict XV. The words of Isaias (60:1) apply to the young man who unconditionally surrendered his life to the "foolishness" and the hidden power of the Father's love in Jesus' saving Cross: *Arise, be enlightened, O Jerusalem; for thy light is come, and the glory of the Lord is risen upon thee.* Gabriel calls out to each of us to say in our hearts, "I will follow you, Lord!" and then to do as he did so well–live out the Gospel and the message of the Cross–perseveringly to the end, accompanied at all times and in all ways—all along the way by Our Lady, Mary, immersed in her Immaculate and maternal Heart.

Reflections on
Saint Gabriel's Journey

Walk while you have the light,
that the darkness overtake thee not.
And he that walks in darkness,
knows not where he goes.
While you have the light, believe in the light
that you may become children of light.
(John 12:35-36)

Chapter One

Vanity and Seeing God's Greater Design

Gabriel slowly realized that the search for lasting peace was not in the passing glamour of the things of this world—but in the possession of God within the heart.

Opening Prayer
Father,...Let sin never ensnare us with empty promises of passing joy.
Make us one with You always, so that our joy may be holy,
and our love may give life.
(Fourteenth Sunday in Ordinary Time, *Roman Sacramentary*)

It was another elegant party at the Pannechetti household, a well-respected Spoletan family. Their daughter, Maria, was Gabriel's close friend during his youth. Maria danced with Gabriel, led by his famed, classical style which he added to the newly introduced popular waltz. The ladies' gowns, overflowing with material and decorated with vibrant-colored bows and ruffles added a dream-like aura to the night.

When the evening came to a close, Gabriel, along with his brother, Michael, and sister, Teresa (nicknamed "Teta"), decided to walk home rather than use the family coach. The spring night was a beautiful one and there was a full moon. Upon reaching their home, Teta burst into tears. She noticed that her valuable brooch was missing. It was a gift from her fiancé! She remembered having seen it on her gown during the walk home. It must have fallen off along the country path they had taken.

Teta was beside herself, crying that she would never see the pin again.

Gabriel insisted that Michael and he search for it, retracing their steps. Lanterns in hand, they set out, Teta following—depressed and feeling hopeless about the venture. Tediously the brothers searched. At last, Gabriel spotted in the gravel path by a large overgrown bush, a glittering object in the moonlight. It was the precious brooch! His sister started crying again, this time tears of happiness. Gabriel tenderly placed it in her hands and gently said: "Here it is, Teta..." Suddenly, his voice took on a serious, concerned tone, and he added: "but don't attach your heart so much to these trifles." (Casimiro, *San Gabriele*, p.14).

Consideration
Recall an incident in your life when an object or person somehow caused you to feel beside yourself, totally frazzled or confused, and how you lost a sense of your own centeredness in God.

Pause for Reflection
Inscription for a Sundial

Happy will be the hours which the style indicates, with no time of your life shadowed by a cloud.

Will the present hour, which the short style marks, be, perhaps, the last one of your life?

As the shadows move, the time of your life is measured and those days which they assent in their flight are so many that are swept away from you.

Not all that glitters in the morning shines at night.
(composed by Gabriel as a college student, c. 1853; from Mabel Farnum, *Saint Gabriel*, p.36)

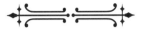

Gabriel must have been thinking about his own "search" for real happiness and peace of soul as he and Michael looked assiduously along the path for their sister's brooch. Teresa's anxiety for it reflected Gabriel's *own* obsession with the right fashion, and the many pleasures of the Spoletan nightlife. He enjoyed engaging in the sophisticated conversations at the salons and attending the countless operas.

It was not these things or events that were bad in themselves, but the energy and worry put into acquiring or having them at all costs. Gabriel had recently witnessed how death quickly comes and steals everything earthbound. His brother, Lawrence, had committed suicide in Rome. Another brother, Paul, so young and handsome in his military uniform, never returned home—dying suddenly of food poisoning. Above all, his beloved sister, Maria-Louise, was swiftly taken away from the family by the cholera epidemic! In the end, he mused, would his vain preoccupations with material things and good times really matter?

Gabriel felt it was time to go deeper under the layers of possessions and entertainment. He began to perceive that everything God blesses us with is good but it is the attitude we approach them with that is crucial. If God is at the center of our hearts, then we will see all of life's gifts and pleasures as graces from him, not as vain objects to be possessed and treasured. ***People will not be used for what they want, but loved for whom they are.*** Talents, fortune, loved ones ...*these are all gifts of love from God.*

Rooted in God, with a profound faith awareness of the Spirit's outpouring love within our very core of being, vanity's hold on us is crushed. We can see everything in perspective and learn to appreciate both people and objects; we can also "let go" and "move on" if it is part of God's will for us; our visions and lives are firmly built on the Lord's certain, abiding presence, we will find lasting peace in Him, and ponder with serenity the never-ending life to come. Quite simply, our lives and thoughts are no longer enslaved by anything or anyone. Gabriel's poetry, composed while in college, and his comment to Teta, were vital reflections of these eternal truths.

The Word of God

Lay not up to yourselves treasures on earth: where the rust and moth consume and where thieves break through and steal. But lay up to your-selves treasures in Heaven where neither the rust nor the moth consumes, and where thieves do not break through and steal. (Matt. 6:19-21)

Closing Prayer

Lord, Thou hast been our refuge from generation to generation. Be-fore the mountains were made and the earth and the world was formed: from eternity and to eternity Thou art God. Thou hast said: be converted, O ye sons of Men. For a thousand years in Thy sight are as yesterday which is past.

And as a watch in the night, things that are counted as nothing, shall their years be. In the morning man shall grow up like grass; in the morn-ing he shall flourish and pass away: in the evening he shall fall, grow dry and wither... the days of our years in them are threescore and ten years... Who knows the power of Thy anger, and for Thy fear can number Thy wrath? So make Thy right hand known and men learned in heart, in wisdom.... We are filled in the morning with Thy mercy: and we have rejoiced, and are delighted all our days. We have rejoiced for the days which Thou hast humbled us: for the years in which we have seen evils. Look upon Thy servants and upon their works: and direct their children. And let the brightness of the Lord our God be upon us: and direct Thou the works of our hands over us; yea, the work of our hand do Thou di-rect.

(Psalm 89...1-6, 10, 12, 14-17)

For Further Reflection
Forsaking Vanity:
Seeing and Living Anew in and Through God

+ Write down a list of things you think you must have to make you happy. Think about them one by one. What makes them so special? Can you live without them peacefully? How does Jesus' love and His Gospel relate to having these particular things, if at all? How could they serve the Kingdom of God? Are they mere vainglories, or are they really mean-ingful in God's grace?

+ Discuss in a small prayer group, or consider alone: many are obsessed with sensual materialistic slogans and advertisements of the modern media. What kind of power do these ads have over you? What do these billboard, television and magazine "images" impress upon your mind? Are our identities built upon such images, consciously or unconsciously, or on the Gospel and Cross of Jesus?

+ Place a picture of a beloved deceased person in your hands as you sit quietly in prayer. In the spirit of the "Communion of Saints," speak to that person who is very near to you in the Lord. Ask him or her to guide you as you journey on earth, to help you see life in perspective, using the gift of time and all your talents according to God's plans for you.

+ Ask the Blessed Mother in a decade of the Rosary to help you reflect on how you give gifts. Are gifts ever a substitute for caring words and deeds to another? Consider how Mary gave her whole self in aiding Saint Elizabeth during the last months of her aged cousin's expectancy.

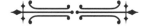

Chapter Two

Placing Difficult Decisions in God's hands

Gabriel struggled with the many choices in life that surrounded him; he was unable to make important decisions. However, through Gabriel's genuine soul-searching and persevering prayer, God's call and purpose for him was finally understood.

Opening Prayer

Conduct me, O Lord, in Thy way, and I will walk in Thy truth: let my heart rejoice that it may fear Thy Name. I will praise Thee, O Lord, my God, with my whole heart, and I will glorify Thy Name forever.

(Ps. 86:11-12)

Gabriel often sat atop Monte Luco, overlooking the city of Spoleto. It was one of his favorite spots. He often did his skilled bird whistles, and with remarkable patience, was able to coax a few songbird friends to his outstretched hand. (Burke, *Happy Was My Youth*, p.29) He felt close to God as he joyed in nature and its creatures. In August, 1856, he was most likely there deep in thought, softly whistling to the birds and pondering over the events which led to his final decision to join the Congregation of the Passion.

Gabriel remembered them all ... In 1851, a grave illness attacked him as an adolescent, and in his religious fervor, the fourteen-year-old promised God to became a religious if he were to be well again. (Zecca, *Lettere Familiari Ed Altri Scritti*, p.181) He recovered but soon forgot

AT THE CROSS WITH MARY

the promise in the vigor and excitement of youthful life. In 1854, when he nearly died from a throat infection, and he experienced what he believed was a cure through the intercession of the newly beatified Jesuit martyr, Andrew Bobola. Gabriel made another "deal" with God, this time applying to the Jesuit Society. (Ibid, p.184) Soon after, he realized it was a hasty decision and rescinded it. A third time, when a stray bullet in a hunting accident could have killed him, but luckily only grazed his nose, he repeated the promise to become a religious, but again didn't keep his promise.

Gabriel had not been making mature responses to his vocation. Intelligent and sharp-witted as he was, he must have come to realize that a relationship with God is a matter of God's grace and our response; it is not based on fear or on idle promises.

Gabriel's saving quality at this difficult and misguided time was his **consistent love for God, the Eucharist, and Mary**. His charity, especially helping the poor, marked his profound sincerity. Also, his desperate promises also revealed a psychological dimension–his legitimate struggle between numerous difficult choices and, as he would later reveal in his letters, temptation to worldly glory–and even sin. Now, praying on Monte Luco, and looking back on all the indecision, Gabriel gratefully acknowledged that Mary's voice was God's mouthpiece in his vocation. Gabriel's prayers for guidance were heard. On August 22, 1856, during the procession of Mary's icon, Gabriel felt the Virgin Mary's voice unmistakably penetrate his heart to follow his deepest purpose–to be a consecrated religious. This would be his way, his vocation. Gabriel now prayed for the perseverance, strength and joy to appreciate and live the vocation he received, making the response uniquely his own.

Consideration
Do I deeply pray for God's will to be done in whatever difficult decisions I am struggling to make?

Pause for Reflection
"My brother, will, perhaps, that happy and blessed hour come to you as it has come to me, even though I am more unworthy than you? Do you not believe that she who is called Refuge of Sinners will turn her merciful eyes upon us? I hope so, and, if it be so, nothing more remains for me to say save 'Arise, and come!!' Do not follow my example who, although called by Our Lord, went on from day to day, procrastinating. No–but if a Voice should call you, do not for an instant doubt nor weigh words. Cast behind your knowledge, relatives and the world, and **put your hand to the work**."

(Excerpt of a letter written by Gabriel to his brother, Michael, who was interested in knowing more about a religious vocation. Eventually Michael would respond to God's call by becoming a medical doctor, husband and father. From Farnum, *Saint Gabriel*, p.111.)

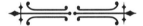

Gabriel's first two vocational decisions were frustrated because he made them out of desperation in sickness and in his own perception of what he thought God required of him. His third unfulfilled promise to consecrate himself to God's service was based on the aftermath of a fearful experience–a near brush with death, and maybe he was goaded by guilt at not keeping his former promises. It was only after acutely listening in prayer and attending to the events of his life, especially the profound loss of his beloved sister, Louisa, that he heard the clear and true call to follow a particular path. Furthermore, it was a total surprise to Gabriel! The call was unlike anything he had formerly planned or envisioned. The Passionists, the congregation he chose, had never been part of his life before this. They were far away from his home; this small group of men were extremely poor, and without a strong scholastic emphasis—everything different from what his present Jesuit teachers exemplified. Yet, the call was of God. God surprises us when we actually predispose ourselves to listen to what HE is trying to tell us. The road map for the life that God stretches out before us to study may be mysterious, far-reaching, and even confusing at first, but it leads to new life in Jesus' power and love.

The Word of God
May the God of our Lord Jesus Christ, the Father of glory, give unto you the spirit of wisdom and revelation, in the knowledge of Him: the eyes of your heart enlightened that you may know what the hope is of His calling, and what are the riches of the glory of His inheritance in the saints. And what is the exceeding greatness of His power toward us who believe according to the operation of the might of His power, which He wrought in Christ, raising Him up from the dead, and setting Him on His right hand in the heavenly places. (Ephesians 1:16-19)

Closing Prayers
For Enlightenment

Lord, You have proved me, and known me: You have known my sitting down and my rising up. You have understood my thoughts afar off: my path and my line You have searched out. And You have foreseen all my ways: for there is no speech in my tongue. Behold, O Lord, You have known all things, the last and those of old: You have formed me, and laid Your hand upon me. Your knowledge has become wonderful to me: it is high, and I cannot reach to it.... You have protected me from my mother's womb. I will praise You, for You are fearfully magnified: wonderful are Your works, and my soul knows right well. My bone is not hidden from You, which You have made in secret: and my substance in the lower parts of the earth. Your eyes saw my imperfect being, and in Your book all shall be written: days shall be formed and no one in them. But to me Your friends, O God, are made exceedingly honorable: their principality is exceedingly strengthened. I will number them, and they shall be multiplied above the sand: I rose up and am still with You.... Prove me, O God, and know my heart: examine me and know my paths. And see if there be in me the way of iniquity: and lead me in the eternal way.
(Psalm 138: 1-6, 13-18, 23-24)

The Prayer of Saint Francis before the Crucifix of San Damiano
All-highest, glorious God, cast Your light into the darkness of my heart.

Give me right faith, firm hope, perfect charity and profound humility, with wisdom and perception, O Lord, so that I may do what is truly Your holy will. Amen.

(From Miller, *In the Footsteps of Saint Clare, A Pilgrim's Guide Book*, p. 97.)

For Further Reflection
Decisions with and for Christ

+ In a solitary night vigil before a cross, place any important decision you must make in the Sacred Heart of Jesus. Ask Him to direct your choice of action in its regard, and to reveal the path He has prepared for you at this stage of your life.

+ Recall that a novena is a truly Biblical way of prayer, reflecting the nine days of the Apostles' and Mary's prayer in the Cenacle before Pentecost. Create a scripturally based novena of prayer to the Holy Spirit; entreat the Spirit to reveal to your mind and heart your specific purpose and mission during your life.

+ Talk about decision-making problems with a trust-worthy friend or mentor who can objectively guide you. See this sharing time as prayer itself. Listen within it to the voice of God.

+ How does Saint Gabriel's vocation story touch you? In what way does he inspire your emulation in answering whatever call you are personally experiencing?

+ List your conflicting choices on paper. Write the pros and cons of each. Put the paper away and spend some time in quiet, restful prayer everyday. In a few days review the list. Can you add to it or eliminate some choices? Continue praying about them, and seeking Christ's light in your final decision.

+ Watch the film *The Passion of the Christ*. As you watch, listen to the call of Our Lord in your life, vocation, and important decision-making: *If you want to be My disciple, take up your cross and follow Me.*

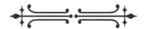

Chapter Three

Risking The Unknown Journey

Without any assurance except his own inner faith and conviction that God was calling him to a particular place and a mission on behalf of the Gospel message, Gabriel left everything familiar and comfortable that was his former world. He risked an unknown future for love of Christ.

Opening Prayer
Lord, You are my Saviour, Brother, and Friend;
guide me in all the travels and changes of my life.
You know where You are taking me as I place my hand in Yours.
Let Your Cross be a light unto my path, a guide unto my feet.
I follow Your call to service and to love.
Wherever I go, O Lord, You are my hope and my delight!

On September 6, 1856, Gabriel left Spoleto and began his journey to the Passionist novitiate in Morravale. His brother, a Dominican priest, who was home on holiday, was asked by their father, Judge Possenti, to accompany Gabriel. All along the route, at various planned resting stations, relatives were notified by letter, pre-written by the judge, and dutifully handed over to them by Father Louis. Judge Possenti's plan was obviously to use these letters to alert the family of the harsh life that Gabriel was about to embrace, impress upon them the great mistake it was for the youth, and request that they test the young man further and try to convince him to return home.

Not only did Gabriel have to face these annoying intrusions and exhausting encounters, but he must have been pondering the fact that he had received no acceptance letter from the Passionist provincial regarding his application for the novitiate. Gabriel had no idea that the provincial had indeed written in the affirmative–but that his father had kept the letter from him. Furthermore, due to Gabriel's obligations as the main speaker for the College's Awards Night, he realized he was already about a week late for the postulancy, the period of preparation before receiving the habit of the novice. He quickly wrote a second letter of explanation to the Passionists, but there was no answer. (Actually, the provincial's second reply came to Spoleto only after Gabriel had departed.) At first, Gabriel must have reasoned that the post was often delayed and sometimes even lost and that the letter of acceptance was, in all likelihood, sent out to him. He had no idea what the Passionists were thinking or if they still expected him. In the end, his worrying turned to peace as he surrendered to trusting simply in the heavenly Father.

Father Louis, seated next to Gabriel atop the stagecoach, was the first to test his brother's vocation. As a friar and a young priest who knew both the joys and sacrifices of religious life and priesthood, he had much to offer in this discussion. Louis was quickly satisfied with the knowledge and faith which Gabriel expressed in terms of the Passionist life to which he aspired. On September 7, in the late evening, the two brothers arrived in the pilgrimage town of the Holy House of Loreto. It was too late to call on their uncle, the Vicar General of Loreto, Canon Acquacotta, and the inns were all full with the vast number of pilgrims who had come to celebrate the feast of Mary's Nativity on the following day.

Making matters worse, there was a terrible rainstorm. Gabriel and Louis finally took refuge in a hospice for the poor. Straw mats were given to them and after they placed them on the floor of the communal hallway, they slowly managed to fall asleep. It was Gabriel's first taste of poverty.

In the morning, on the Virgin Mary's birthday, Gabriel spent an intense period of adoration and prayer in the sacred house at Loreto, which is believed to be the Holy Family's dwelling, and is revered within the great structure of the basilica. The discomfort of the previous night hadn't dismayed Gabriel. Louis later wrote in a letter that he "found him kneeling quietly in a corner, completely absorbed in prayer." (Burke, *Happy Was My Youth,* p. 77)

Later in the morning, Gabriel made a general confession of his whole life to one of the priests on duty. This sacrament of reconciliation was to be one of the highlights of his spiritual life. It gave added peace and joy to his vocational decision. He felt cleansed of past frivolities and sinfulness and ready to approach a new kind of life. Gabriel then attended his own brother's Mass and received Communion. He was more than ready now to face the challenge his uncle would present him with at the noonday meal in the vicar's residence. The canon was very impressed by his nephew's maturity in responding politely, yet firmly to all his questions and their many-sided angles of argumentation. Gabriel was not to be frightened by images of a rough penitential life. The youth, while showing a true humility, was not at all intimidated by his prestigious uncle. Gabriel spoke from his heart and his zeal won the canon over to his side.

Finally, on September 9, Louis and Gabriel passed through their mother's town, Civatanova, and there made a brief visit with her relatives. When they discovered Gabriel's destiny, they were shocked; the Passionists were too strict for him. He would never endure their diet. Their rough, wool habits were uncomfortable, and their hours for prayers were excessive. Gabriel had to repeat the same reasons all over again regarding his decision. He was trying not to lose his patience. The disturbing visit came to an end and the final stop before actually reaching the Passionists was to be at a Capuchin Friary where another uncle, Father John Baptist Frisciotti, was the guardian.

This holy, and very amiable person was obligated to test Gabriel's vocation in respect to his sister's husband's request. The gentle Franciscan noted the shine in Gabriel's eyes and the goodness of his eager nephew. Father John Baptist's questioning was kind and concerned. After a shared lunch, he told Louis that he would walk with them the five miles to the novitiate and present Gabriel to the rector of Our Lady of the Oaks Retreat.

The three men cheerfully hiked the path leading to the red-tiled roof and white-walled monastery. Interestingly, a son of Saint Dominic and one of Saint Francis were escorting the future saint of the family of Blessed Paul of the Cross. In the distance, Gabriel could see the monastic belfry rising. What emotions must have stirred in Gabriel's heart at the sight of it! The Passionists were indeed waiting for the Grand Assessor's son, and Gabriel was warmly welcomed to his new home. It had been a long, arduous and emotionally draining journey to this place, but now the struggles all fell into place. He experienced profound joy. The God of love had led him in the right paths. He could sincerely pray and continue to hope, *He is faithful, Who has called you, Who also will do it.* (I Thess. 5:24) On September 21, Gabriel, who had been known as Francis Joseph Possenti since his birth, received the black habit of penance and his new name. He wrote to his father: "The day has come at last! For a long time Almighty God was waiting for me, but I ungratefully remained deaf to his call...But the infinite mercy of God wisely arranged all for the best. Today, the feast of Our Lady of Sorrows, our mother and patron, to my indescribable happiness I was clothed in the religious habit, taking the name Confrater Gabriel of the Sorrowful Virgin." (Burke, Ibid, p. 92)

Consideration
"Go in peace, for you will be well escorted; for He Who created you has provided for your sanctification, and after He created you, He infused into you His Holy Spirit. He has ever guarded you as a loving mother does her little child."

(Fran Hickey, O.S.C., *Clare of Assisi, Friend of Francis, Bride of Christ,* p.55)

Pause for Reflection
Lead, kindly light, amid the encircling gloom.
Lead thou me on.
The night is dark and I am far from home.
Lead thou me on.
Keep thou my feet, I do not ask to see
The distant scene, one step enough for me.

I was not ever thus, nor prayed that Thou
Should lead me on.
I loved to choose and see my path, but now
Lead thou me on.

AT THE CROSS WITH MARY

I loved the garish day, and, spite of fears,
Pride ruled my will, remember not past years.

So long thy power hath blest me, sure it still
Will lead me on
O'er moor and fen, o'er crag and torrent, till
The night is gone,

And with the morn those angel faces smile,
Which I have loved long since, and lost awhile.

(Venerable Cardinal Newman, From Kelly, S.J, *Youth Before God*, p.96)

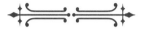

Gabriel traveled four harrowing days, not knowing for certain what the end of the road would hold for him. His faith encouraged him with a sense that if he had not responded then and there to the call of God, he would not be able to humanly find the courage to do so at a later date. In today's world, it is not easy to go against the majority opinion or the plans set up for someone by their own family. However, in the mid nineteenth century, a close-knit high class Italian family had even more psychological control over the fate of their offspring. In light of this, Gabriel's trip was a radical move of independence; it would not have been possible for him unless he had been totally convinced that he was being true to God's plans. Gabriel was enabled by the Spirit, in spite of the lack of both paternal approval, and any visible proof of being accepted by the Passionists. In the face of rebuffs and arguments from his own relatives, he forged on

to his goal while maintaining peace within himself. Here again, we can truly see a parallel to the life of Saint Francis of Assisi who abandoned himself to God the Father at the cost of losing his earthly father and at the expense of public ridicule. Both Gabriel and Francis of Assisi took enormous risks but found that God was right there, immediately ready to embrace them and seal their lives in His tender love.

So often the ability and courage to risk an unusual project and to follow through on what may be inspired by the Holy Spirit is lacking. We become paralyzed by the fear of what others, especially family and peers may think about us. Our dreams may be labeled foolish or imprudent! Unfortunately, we may become stuck in a spiritual quagmire. On the other hand, risking oneself for God's kingdom will always mean personal growth, as well as Gospel light for the many we encounter along the journey! The risk for Christ and for love of Him can only promise us, in spite of the inevitable personal passion and crosses we will have to bear, a deeper trust and union with Him. Perhaps, in the middle of, or toward the end of our journey, we will understand a meaning and purpose to our call that is even more profound then what we initially envisioned: *And we know that to them who love God all things work together unto good, to such as, according to His purpose, are called to be saints.* (Romans 8:28).

The Word of God
And Jesus walking by the Sea of Galilee saw two brothers, Simon who is called Peter, and Andrew, his brother, casting a net into the sea (for they were fishermen). And He said to them: "Come after Me and I will make you fishers of men." And they immediately leaving their nets, followed Him. And going on from thence, He saw two other brothers, James, the son of Zebedee, and John his brother, in a ship with Zebedee their father, mending their nets: and He called them. And they forthwith left their nets and their father, and followed Him. (Matthew 4: 18-21)

Closing Prayer
For The Journey

The Lord is my Shepherd, and I shall want nothing.
He has set me in a place of pasture.
He has brought me up on the waters of refreshment:
He has converted my soul.

He has led me on the paths of justice, for His own Name's sake.
For though I should walk in the midst of the shadow of death,
I will fear no evil, for You are with me.
Your rod and Your staff, they have comforted me.
You have prepared a table before me against those that afflict me.
You have anointed my head with oil: and my chalice inebriated me, how
goodly it is! And Your mercy will follow me all the days of my life.
And that I may dwell in the house of the Lord unto length of days.

(Psalm 22)

You are the light of the world. A city seated on a mountain cannot be
hid. Neither do men light a candle and then put it under a bushel basket
but upon a candlestick that it may shine to all in the house. So let your
light shine before men that they may see your good deeds and glorify your
Father Who is in Heaven.

(Matthew 5:14-16)

For Further Reflection
Following the Way

+ Do you recall a crossroad in your life journey when some circumstance or person convinced you to change directions? Do you see God's best designs in the final outcome or do you think that the original plans were somehow blocked, ruined or compromised? Bring whatever feelings you may have to Jesus and ask Him to bless, and/or heal all that transpired and to direct your future steps.

+ Give thanks to God for the loved ones and the leaders in your life who risked a lot for the sake of a cause they believed in and who have made great contributions to your family or community. Do something special for one of them, or simply let them know of your appreciation.

+ In what way does Gabriel inspire or teach you to react to the well-intentioned but misguided advice of family and/or friends that opposes the very core of what you are?

+ Write in your journal all your fears about spiritually-related projects you always think about doing, e.g.: time away for a retreat, volunteer work with the disabled, etc.—but which you can't seem to act upon.

Speak to the Virgin Mary about these fears while thinking about her acts of courage and charity for others in the Gospels.

+ Meditate upon a crucifix, seeking insight, light and grace to follow Jesus wherever He leads you.

+ In difficult moments of the faith journey, fear may overtake your initial courage; remember Jesus calmed the very seas. Passionist Father, Malcolm Cornwell, C.P., writes a phrase in his book *Praying the Passion, Living the Gospel* a beneficial reminder to repeat in our quiet time, as well as in our moments of fear: "Wind, water, and wayfaring hearts all become calm in the presence of the One Who says, 'It is I; do not be afraid.'"

+ Father Peter Lechner, S.P., writes that, "It could be said that the Our Father with its petition 'Thy will be done' and 'give us this day our daily bread' is an ideal prayer for the Gift of Counsel." (*Gifts of the Holy Spirit, Priestly People*, p. 4) Try this prayer as a true petition for guidance.

AT THE CROSS WITH MARY

Chapter Four

Completely God's

Gabriel completely surrendered his life to God's love. He lived a penitential life like an athlete preparing for victory. Unlike an athlete however, his goal was to possess and to be possessed by Christ. Like Saint John the Baptist, he lived the words of dedication to Jesus: *He that has the bride is the bridegroom: but the friend of the bridegroom, who stands and hears him, rejoices with joy because of the bridegroom's voice. This my joy therefore is fulfilled. He must increase, but I must decrease.*

(John 3:29)

Opening Prayer:
Take, O Lord, everything–my entire liberty, my understanding, my will.
All that I am and all I have received is a gift from You.
I give it all back to You, my Jesus, that You may do with it whatever You will. Give me only Your love and Your grace!
With these, I am rich enough and there is nothing else I desire.
(Saint Ignatius of Loyola)

After a novitiate year of intense happiness for "Confrater Gabriel of the Sorrowful Virgin," the time for his perpetual vows approached. His father made yet another attempt at persuading his son to return home; he communicated to Gabriel's Capuchin uncle, Father John Baptist, to speak with Gabriel again. The Franciscan relative had made the short hike several times this past year to visit with his nephew at the novitiate. Again, faithful to his brother-in-law's request, he went to the monastery, and as usual, found Gabriel extremely happy and resolved to make his vows; the friar related this to Sante Possenti by mail. Burke acutely observes that, "This was more than another attempt to try Gabriel's vocation. This was the desperate effort of a lonely old man to win back at the eleventh hour a son whom he had reluctantly surrendered to God." (*Happy Was My Youth*, p.117) Gabriel wrote home, " I well remember, dearest father, that I promised you to return home whenever I was sure that the Lord had not called me to join this Congregation. But, father dear, how can I possibly leave so good a Master as Jesus Christ, so loving a mother as Mary?" (Ibid.)

On the day of Profession, September 22, 1857, the young man who lay prostrate on the stone floor of the chapel, covered by a black funeral pall to denote his death to the world's sin and false promises, was a person in the exciting process of true transformation in the Spirit. When he rose from the ground, he knelt before the superior to profess the three evangelical vows of poverty, chastity, and obedience, and a fourth unique vow–first made by the founder, Paul of the Cross–to promote devotion to the Passion of Jesus in his heart and in the hearts of the faithful. Even before this moment, he had been eagerly learning in the novitiate year to apply these vows, making them a daily and living part of himself.

The badge and emblem of the Passion was then clipped on the black habit over his chest. Gabriel listened to the important meaning of the words being read to him: "...Lord God, we beseech You through the merits of Jesus Christ, grant that this sign of the life-giving Passion which Your servant will wear externally on his breast may be graven deeply on his heart. Grant him the grace and the mortification of the Cross, ever to live in Jesus Christ, so that he may be able to imprint this sign also on the hearts of the faithful and spread amongst them devotion to the Passion of Your Son." (Burke, p.120) After the ceremony, Gabriel wrote home again: "...Such a grace, father dear, can never be sufficiently appreciated. Since I have been thus privileged by God, the obligation of corresponding with this grace continuously increases. I'll leave you to imagine how great is my need for your prayers, and the prayers of others, too." (Ibid., p.121) Saint Gabriel, the first Passionist canonized after the holy founder, Paul of the Cross, truly immersed himself in the founder's spirituality of becoming "lost in God, Who is charity, Who is all love..." and living his exhortation: "Oh, how much you must be humble, charitable with everybody, meek, patient, having a good opinion of all...Oh, how much you must be a friend of silence, of remaining secluded, of fleeing idleness, of working and being silent in order to remain interiorly united with God...." (Martin Bialis, C.P., *The Mysticism of the Passion in Saint Paul of the Cross*, pp.204, 206).

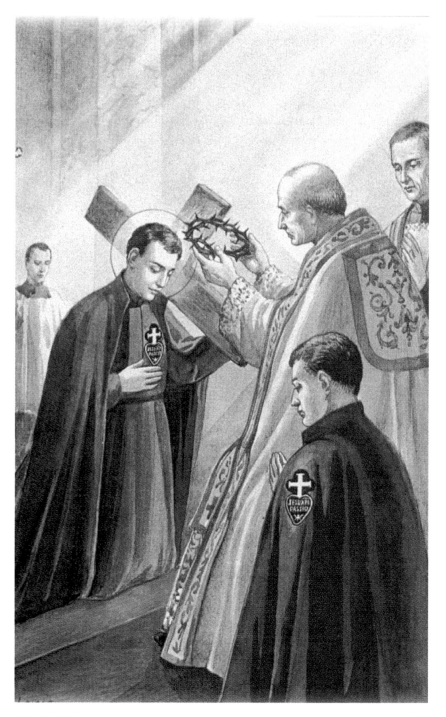

Consideration

*"Sincerely examine the way you are following the Master.
Ask yourself if your self-surrender is of a dry officious type, with a faith
that has no sparkle to it; if there is humility or sacrifice, or any good
works throughout your day; if you are all show and pay no attention to
the details of each moment...In a word, if you lack Love. If this is the
case your ineffectiveness should come at no surprise to you. React right
away, and be led by the hand of Our Lady."*

(Saint Josemaria Escriva, *From The Forge*, p.335)

Pause for Reflection

Saint Gabriel's Prayer to the Father for Total Conversion

O Lord, behold me here at Your feet to implore Your mercy and pardon. Would You suffer any loss by granting me a great love for You, deep humility, great purity of heart, soul and body, true fraternal charity, great sorrow for having offended You and the grace never to offend You again?... To obtain it, I offer You the merits of Jesus Christ, my Redeemer. My Lord, I am a poor person: I have no merits of my own. But behold my merits: *Vulnera tua merita mea!* (Your wounds are my merit!) If for love of You, I had shed the blood which Your Son has shed for me, would You not grant me this grace? How much more will You grant it to me when Your blessed Son has shed His own Blood for me. Didn't You promise in the Gospel to grant me all that I ask of You for the good of my soul? *Ask and you shall receive.* Since this is so, You cannot go back upon Your word. For this reason, I place all my trust in You: graciously hear me. I ask You to hear my prayer through Your infinite goodness, through the Heart of Your Son, wounded for love of me and His Most Precious Blood and merits, through the infinite love of the Eternal Spirit, through the love You have for Your daughter Mary, and in honor of the whole Heavenly Court, into which I ask You, one day, to also receive me. Amen."

(from Ceci, Scritti di *S. Gabriele dell'Addolorata,
Studente Passionista*, pp.169-179)

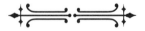

Gabriel's willing embrace of the mortifications of the Passionist Rule–
the short hours of sleep on the uncomfortable straw mat, the meager food,
the always bare, roughly sandaled-feet, and the long periods of fasting–

were but a means to an end: to free himself of the pitfalls of a life otherwise ruled by selfishness, mediocrity, misdirected sensuality, greed, and hunger for power and prestige. In place of the unsettling dependence on outside influences of things, persons, and events, Gabriel assiduously aimed at refocusing on the Trinitarian love within him, making God the anchor and motivating factor of his life. To enter into such an intense and loving unity with God's life and love, a discipline and purification of the disciple had to regularly take place. Bad habits and ungodly desires needed to be removed. Penance, prudently guided by his spiritual director, permitted Gabriel to do just that on a day to day basis–and to gradually emerge a new man of Christ, completely God's!

It was not an easy process; Gabriel had to truly work at Christian growth! His faith-life was often dry and without any consolation. He suffered from enormous temptations against God and the life of celibacy. There were times he felt that a darkness covered his very soul. (Poage, *Son of the Passion*, p.71) Prayer, spiritual guidance, and the penitential life helped him through the interior storms.

There was another problem, though. Impulsive and emotional as he was, Gabriel, at first over extended his need for external penitential acts. Fr. Norbert swiftly corrected him. Norbert eventually wrote to Gabriel's father about Gabriel's acts of penance: "The mistake he made at the beginning ... has been replaced by reasonable prudence...he knows for himself that there can be too much of a good thing and is aware of the traps and snares of the evil one." (Burke, p. 153) The former spoiled and often hot-tempered son of the eminent jurist of Spoleto was now happily scouring pots in the kitchen, putting up with or even befriending those with irritating personalities, and willing himself to be less distracted in his preparatory studies for the priesthood. His penance had necessarily evolved into a truer form, a discipline and expansion of his thoughts, attitudes and emotions in the Gospel spirit.

Gabriel seized countless little opportunities to divest himself of whatever was in him that was contrary to Jesus' "Good News" in order to clothe himself with Christ as Saint Paul writes: *Put ye on, therefore, as the elect of God, holy and beloved, the bowels of mercy, benignity, humility, modesty, patience....* (Colossians 3:12,14) Once, going to Father Norbert, he knelt down and with unusual feeling, and told the priest, "Father, do you know of anything in me that is not pleasing to God? Tell me and I will root it out at any cost!" Norbert tried to relax the obvious anxiety of his spiritual son, but at the same time he was amazed at the young man's sincerity and candid desire to please God. Gabriel added: "Everything in me must go that is not for God!" (Poage, p.102) This penetrating statement of surrender of negative forces and egotistical desires shows his soul yearning for God to become all light and all love within it.

The Word of God

I beseech you, therefore, brethren, by the mercy of God, that you present your bodies a living sacrifice, holy, pleasing unto God, your reasonable service. And be not conformed to this world; but be reformed in the newness of your mind, that you may prove what is the good, and the acceptable, and the perfect will of God.

(Romans 12:1-2)

I would rather, by Divine Mercy, be the least among the Passionists than be the son of the king and heir to the kingdom.

(Saint Gabriel of the Most Sorrowful Virgin)

Closing Prayer
Of Surrender To God

Father, I abandon myself into Your hands; do with me what You will. Whatever You may do, I thank You: I am ready for all, I accept all. Let only Your will be done in me, and in all your creatures. I wish no more than this, O Lord.

Into Your hands I commend my soul; I offer it to You with all the love of my heart, for I love You, Lord, and so need to give myself, to surrender myself into Your hands, without reserve, and with boundless confidence, for You are my Father.

(Blessed Charles de Foucauld, from Caretto,
Summoned by Love, p. 19)

For Further Reflection
Giving Self to God

+ If you are a religious or a priest, spend peaceful reflection time remembering the day of your vow-taking or when the bishop placed his hands over your head, or the moment your hands were anointed with chrism. Pray with confidence and trust for the renewal of joy and dedication in your call to ministry and contemplation.

+ Married couples can arrange a home Mass to be said where they can share with a few special friends and family members the celebration of their sacramental love. Also, a contract could be written within a private prayer service between the two persons, consecrating their mutual love and partnership to Christ's Kingdom.

+ Those who live a single life-style or are in a unique pure association/ partnership that proclaims God's love may set aside a day to commemorate their baptismal promises and the anointing they received in holy oils as kingly, priestly, and holy people of God. A written commitment to live out these marvelous aspects of sanctity can be done and kept in a Bible or special place for occasional meditation on the essence and meaning of life in Christ.

+ For young adult Catholics: recall the day of Confirmation. Think about the ritual and the impact the day had on you. How did the Holy Spirit come once again but uniquely to you on this day? What mission was given to you? If your memory is vague read a book on the sacrament of Confirmation and personalize it for yourself. Ask the Holy Spirit to enlighten, confirm, and anoint you anew with spiritual chrism in the love and service of Jesus.

+ What aspects of your Christian day-to-day living do you consider a response to Jesus' call to repentance and conversion? Discuss with your spiritual director or in a group the positive value of penance as a way to a more complete union with God's life in you and with others in your life.

+ Pope John Paul II, wrote: "In the Sacrifice of the Cross, made present anew in every Eucharist, Christ offers Himself for the salvation of the world." (*Gift and Mystery*, p. 80) Consecrate each morning in union with Jesus' sacrifice and offer your day and your life in union to Him anew. In the evening ask yourself, "How have I offered myself to God and His people today?"

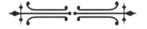

Chapter Five

A Gift for Joy

Confidence and cheerfulness radiated from Gabriel to others—even in the darkest hours of his life; they reflected a man who was in love with Christ and was fully alive in that life-giving love, particularly expressed by Jesus in the outpouring of his Precious Blood.

The obvious aura about Gabriel's person encompassed not only a personal love for Jesus Christ but also a channel of peace and happiness for others. Like Mary's Magnificat, his very being was a Gospel song of praise to the Father. Father Cingolani, C.P., calls Saint Gabriel in his prayer, "Loving saint of the smile."

(Life and Prayers, p.39)

Opening Prayer
Lord God, You gave Saint Gabriel a special privilege of entering into the Passion of Your Son and the Virgin Mary.
Teach us to contemplate with his eyes the very mystery of salvation and to grow in love in the spirit of joy.
Grant this through Christ our Lord. Amen.
(Passionist Proper Offices, *Feast of Saint Gabriel*,
Mid-afternoon Prayer, pp.79-80)

Gabriel's contagious happiness was often commented on by Father Norbert. He wrote, "He had large dark eyes, so lively and expressive ...His whole countenance showed a perennial smile; it was attractive and devout."

(Burke, *Happy was My Youth*, p.199) A fellow student remarked, "He possessed a priceless gift of undisturbed cheerfulness..." (Camillus, *Saint Gabriel, Passionist*, p.147)

Gabriel would become popularly known as "the smiling saint." Father Norbert adds a further pen-picture to describe Gabriel's charm: "He was naturally very talkative, in a friendly way to be sure, always well-spoken and very much to the point, and always in such a pleasant way that everybody liked to listen to him ... he was able to flavor his talk with a touch of salt, a certain piquancy, a delightful touch of humor..." (Ibid, p. 198)

Gabriel's bliss was not ignorant. He understood that life was a gift from God to relish lovingly, to live completely and without reserve, as exemplified in the mystery of Jesus' Precious Blood. Jesus' Blood was the family bond uniting Gabriel to the One Body of the Lord, and making us all "blood brothers and sisters" in the New Covenant. It was the seal of Gabriel's relationship with the Lord. Like the Passionist bishop and saint, Vincent Strambi, Gabriel had a profound appreciation for the Blood of Christ; it was the reason for his confidence and the very exhilaration he showed in living out his Passionist vocation. In 1986, Pope John Paul II remarked that the "Most Precious Blood of our Lord has always been the object of a special attention on the part of all the saints: it is the school of sanctity, of justice, of love…" (Father Peter Nobili, C.PP.S., Editor, *The Precious Blood Family*, p. 20) Since his school days, Gabriel belonged to the Precious Blood Confraternity.

Like his Saviour, Gabriel was compelled to share his joy. When a certain Brother Sylvester painfully struggled with chronic depression, he was recommended by another novice to speak with Confrater Gabriel. Gabriel listened with keen interest and concern. After talking with the brother for a while, he offered the assurance of his prayers to the Blessed Mother, Our Lady of Holy Hope, a special title for Mary among the Passionists. Gabriel went immediately to Mary's altar: the Madonna's portrait above him showed Jesus in her arms and in Christ's hand was the sign of hope–the Holy Cross. Gabriel prayed at length before this image for his needy confrere. The next day, with the assurance received by the inner light received in prayer, Gabriel told Sylvester, "Our Lady of Holy Hope has obtained that favor for you!" There and then, Brother Sylvester's melancholy was remarkably cured for the rest of his life. (Burke, p.105).

Gabriel's joyfulness was also a magnet for Christ, attracting others to the blessedness promised to those who strive to live the beatitudes. Often priests and seminarians from the diocese made their retreats at the Passionist house. Various accounts show that many were drawn to the dignity and contentment observed in Gabriel's demeanor and actions. They wanted to get to know him better and discuss spiritual issues. Inevitably, Norbert would have to contend with their inquiries regarding the student or grant permission to speak with him. Also, the local parish priest's nephew, a medical student by the name of Francis Dionisi, often came to the monastery to pray. Norbert introduced the good student to Gabriel. Francis and Gabriel took walks together and discussed their spiritual lives. Sometimes they sat in the flower garden that Gabriel successfully cultivated. A warm, mutual and supportive friendship developed and lasted until Gabriel's early death. (Ibid, p.225)

These scenes portray neither the flowery image of Saint Gabriel seen in the mass-produced holy cards, nor the remote monk always praying alone in his cell. What we encounter through these small vignettes is a living, very human man, full of God's love, whose joy becomes a healing gift for others.

Consideration

The many faces of our magazine and billboard covers today are often sexually provocative and brooding. Even the happy looks with radiant smiles are undoubtedly connected with products to be purchased and possessed. There is a vast difference between the "joy" these images promise and Jesus' Gospel proclamation to find treasure in the recesses of the human heart.

Pause for Reflection

Gabriel speaks to us in his prayer of confidence in the true source of love: "If God has gone so far as to give His only Son for me, if Jesus Christ has gone so far to sacrifice Himself for me in such a hard and costly way, if He has poured out His Precious Blood so liberally on my behalf, why should I fear that He will withhold the rest from me? It is so much less than what He has already bestowed on me. And have I not also a heavenly

Mother who will look after all my interests with all a mother's care?"
(Saint Gabriel Possenti, from Burke, *Happy Was My Youth*, p.224)

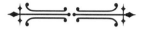

Gabriel's joy was not automatic; it was nurtured. Gabriel experienced mood changes and sadness over events like anybody else. Nonetheless, he strove to pray through moodiness or any unsettling emotions and go beyond them. Among his private resolutions, we find: "I will rejoice at the success of others ... I will close my heart against disquiet of any kind; against sadness and moroseness, and much more against anything like aversion and retaliation ... I will rejoice at the good done by others and will deem it a fault to feel any sentiments of envy or jealousy ... I will try to reproduce in my conduct whatever I see edifying and virtuous in the conduct of my companions." (Mead, *Saint Gabriel, Passionist, A Youthful Gospel Portrait*, pp. 123-125) All his efforts toward deeper joy and appreciation for his life and the life of others paid off immensely. Writing home again to his father, Gabriel's outstanding happiness as a Passionist is evident: "This morning Father Norbert held a conference with me on the beauty and excellence of the religious life. He gave me ideas about it that I never had before...I would rather be a monk in my cell than a king upon his throne." (Burke, p.145)

The Word of God
As the Father has loved Me, I also have loved you. Abide in My love. If you keep My commandments, you shall abide in My love; as I also have kept My Father's commandments, and abide in His love. These things I have spoken to you, that My joy may be in you, and your joy may be filled. This is My commandment, that you love one another as I have loved you. Greater love than this no man has, that a man lay down his life for his friends. You are My friends if you do the things that I command you. I will not now call you servants, for the servant knows not what his lord does. But I have called you friends: because all things whatsoever I have heard of My Father I have made known to you. You have not chosen Me, but I have chosen you: and have appointed you, that you should go, and bring forth fruit, and that your fruit should remain: that whatsoever you shall ask of the Father in My Name, He will give it to you. These things I command you, that you love one another.
(John15: 9-17)

Closing Prayer
Of Joy In Christ

Blessed be the God and Father of our Lord Jesus Christ, Who has blessed us with spiritual blessings in heavenly places in Christ: as He chose us in Him before the foundation of the world, that we should be holy and unspotted in His sight in charity. Who has predestinated us unto the adoption of children through Jesus Christ unto Himself, according to the purpose of His will: unto the praise of the glory of His grace, in which He has graced us in His beloved Son. In Whom we have redemption through His Blood, the remission of sins according to the riches of His grace, which has superabounded in us in all wisdom and prudence, that He might make known unto us the mystery of His will, according to His good pleasure, which He has purposed in Him, in the dispensation of the fullness of times, to re-establish all things in Christ, that are in Heaven and on earth, in Him.

(Ephesians1: 3-10)

For Further Reflection
Dare to be Happy in Christ

+ In a chapel, or some quiet spot outdoors, sit in the presence of the Holy Spirit and draw up your own practical resolutions for enabling your personality to be a sign of Christian joy to others.

+ Creatively write a poem or hymn of praise, expressing personal gratitude in your relationship with Christ.

+ Think about people in your life who are successful and talented. Expand your inner self by taking pleasure in their lives. Allow their happy existence to have a positive effect on your attitudes and way of living.

+ Pray the Joyful Mysteries of the rosary while reading relevant Scripture passages before each decade. Rejoice with Mary over the miracle of the Incarnation of the Word, Jesus—the Fruit of her womb.

+ Your true self is discovered in the sacred and pierced Heart of Jesus Crucified and Risen; there, in Him, ask how you can daily learn to warm and expand your own heart, and share it in your relationships and with the world.

Chapter Six

Proclaiming the Gospel

Saint Gabriel was called to proclaim Jesus to the people. As both an avid student of theology, and a lover of the Gospel, he was determined to preach sermons about Our Lord wherever he could and by whatever means were available to him. In love with the Saviour, Gabriel was compelled to tell all the wonders of Christ's redeeming love.

Opening Prayer
I will always hope; and will add to all Thy praise. My mouth shall show forth Thy justice; Thy salvation all the day long. Because I have not known learning I will enter into the power of the Lord: O Lord, I will be mindful of Thy justice alone. Thou hast taught me, O God, from my youth; and till now I will declare Thy wonderful works.
(Psalm 70: 14—17)

Preparing for the priesthood, Gabriel wrote, "We cannot labor fruitfully in the Lord's vineyard unless we have previously acquired a goodly store of learning and sanctity." (Burke, *Happy Was My Youth*, p.138) Gabriel studied well and his letters and prayers bear the mark of one who read the scriptures and tried to inculcate their meaning into one's life. He prayed with all his heart. And he burned to share the truth of Christ's saving love. He had no intention of waiting for ordination to preach but knew that he was to commence the proclamation of the kingdom at once.

Gabriel found a pleasing method to involve his fellow students in theological discussion that would lead all to be mutually inspired. Father Norbert astutely observed Gabriel's innate gift for spreading the message of salvation and readily gave the seminarian permission to engage in apostolic works.

Gabriel pursued teaching catechism to the simple shepherd children. He was very successful with his young charges. He taught them the basic tenets of the Catholic faith and prepared them for the sacraments. He asked them to pass this knowledge along to their parents. He taught them to pray, giving them simple instructions of how to do so even as they tended the sheep. At times when the seminarians led the rosary or gave ferverinos in the public chapel, the townspeople were particularly attracted to Gabriel because he seemed so sincere about his love for God. Gabriel lived what he preached! He became special to the people because he was able to bring to them an increased faith that God was with them in their work and family lives. From these simple connections with them, Gabriel was etched into their hearts; long after his death, his memory remained with the country folk, and they passed unto their children the story of his concern and love for them. Two particular accounts illustrate Gabriel's unique ways of proclaiming the Gospel:

One day during a walk in the countryside, a man approached Gabriel and his companions and began to verbally express his dejection and anger.

Reportedly, he was going to give himself up to imprisonment for a crime for which he was unjustly accused. Crying, the man announced his complete innocence. He was taken aside by Gabriel, and they talked together in private for some time. Father Norbert and the other students watched them from a distance. The man's features gradually changed from despair to hope, from anxiety to a look of peace. No doubt Gabriel had preached the crucified Jesus and the unjust accusation pronounced upon Him by the Sanhedrin, and His obedience to the Father's will in all things. Perhaps, Gabriel also revealed some reassuring insight

AT THE CROSS WITH MARY

to the man about the final outcome of his case. Whatever was said, the man was able to move on, *interiorly free* and trusting God's Providence. (Lucas & Alluno, *Gabriele dell'Addolorata*, Sceneggiatura e Disegni, p.87)

At another time in Pievetorina, a certain holy woman, Maria Anna Marucci, who was known for her prayer life and exceptional gift to encourage people with hope and peace, was suddenly dying. She was twenty-nine years old and was in extreme pain from a malignant illness.

Confraters Gabriel and Hermenegild went to visit and console her at her deathbed. Gabriel talked to her about the mystery of Jesus' Cross and the privilege she had of uniting her sufferings in faith with the Lord's own sacrifice. Maria Anna, a person of tried asceticism and already perfected in the Gospel light, understood well the wise seminarian's words. Then Gabriel prayed with and for her that Jesus and Mary would kindly support her and lead her to paradise. Shortly after the brothers' visit, she serenely died on March 31, 1859. (Ibid, p.74)

Consideration
A Jesus story or saying leaps out at us and tells us something that brings life ... When our eyes are opened and our ears unstopped, our mouth is also loosed. We speak back to what first spoke to us...
(Shea, *The Spirit Master*, p. 194)

Pause for Reflection
For we preach not ourselves, but Jesus Christ Our Lord: and ourselves your servants through Jesus. For God Who commanded the light to shine out of darkness, has shined in our hearts to give the light of the knowledge of the glory of God, in the face of Christ Jesus.
(II Cor. 4:5-6)

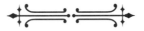

It is clear that Gabriel followed the Saviour's command to preach the love of the Trinity in Jesus' Name to all people. Like the Passionist founder, Paul of the Cross, Gabriel was eager to teach the laity to pray and to develop a prayer life within the context of their own lives. He saw *every encounter* as a potential moment for sharing the Light. By his attentiveness, his care, his words of zeal and conviction, Gabriel had became for others what the holy founder had desired for each of his monks to be: a "living picture of

Jesus Crucified." (Kelly, *Listen to His Love, A Life of Paul of the Cross*, p.177).

Rev. Jean LaFrance exquisitely captures the spirit of proclamation when he writes:

"...Do Christians let others see that today salvation has come to this house, that their bread is nourishing, their joy evident, that the Gospel is light and makes all holy? Sharing the life of all people, you have a special role since non-Christians can glimpse Christ through your own life, for they have to be living signs of salvation. You have to convey your contemplation, your joy, your love and your freedom. The light of the Beatitudes must shine from your face and give light to everyone who sees your life. You have only one thing to do, to draw all women and men into this contemplation of Christ which has gripped you and changed your life....

"You don't convey a formula, an ideology, but a Person, Jesus Christ, a man of joy, peace, light and love. Jesus came to bring the fire of love, not a book. At some point in time, you must say that Jesus is the Saviour.... Above all, take care to talk of Christ at the heart of people's lives. To do this, you don't have to be a hero, an intellectual or a fashion plate, but a saint who is in love with Jesus Christ."

(Pray to Your Father in Secret, pp.63-64)

The Word of God

And going, preach, saying: The kingdom of Heaven is at hand. Heal the sick, raise the dead, cleanse the lepers, cast out devils: freely have you received, freely give...For nothing is covered that shall not be revealed, nor hid that shall not be known. That which I tell you in the dark, speak in the light: and that which you hear in the ear, preach from the housetops.

(Matt. 10: 7-8; 26-27)

Closing Prayer

God, our Father, You will all to be saved and come to know the knowledge of your truth. Send workers into Your great harvest that the Gospel may be preached to every creature and Your people, gathered by the Word of life and strengthened by the power of the sacraments, may advance in the way of salvation and love. We ask this through our Lord Jesus Christ.

(The Roman Missal Sacramentary,
Votive Mass for the Spread of the Gospel)

For Further Reflection
Sharing The Good News

+ Saint Gabriel was baptized at the same ancient font as Saint Francis and Saint Clare of Assisi. Remembering these outstanding citizens of Assisi and their zeal in spreading the love of the Crucified and Risen Jesus, pray intensely to God: "Make *me* a *channel* of Your peace and love!"

+ Discuss with others who share your spiritual journey how your lives can take on a new manifestation of God's liberating love. What projects or plans can you come up with together or on your own, to be a true missionary in your neighborhood? Or how can you revamp the good works you're already involved in to make them more authentic signs of the Risen Lord's presence among His people?

+ Warmly share the Faith today with a child by offering an interesting children's Bible storybook or a coloring book with Gospel scenes. Spend time with the child explaining the pictures or talking about the stories you read. Or share a good spiritual reading that may be helpful or interesting to a friend or relative.

+ Meditate on the Passion of Jesus, asking God for the courage and wisdom to defend your Faith—even if it means possible ridicule or loss of popularity. Also, beg the Holy Spirit for the gift of sensitivity and timing to know how to reach the hearts of others who may be spiritually hungry and searching for God.

+ As you pray about sharing the Catholic Faith, and explaining it well, both study and learn more about the Scriptures with study aides and accompanying scholarly commentary. Know that the Holy Spirit will guide you as you seek to proclaim love—the Lord Jesus. This is a humbling and great responsibility!

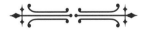

Chapter Seven

humility, Truthfulness Before God

Saint Gabriel chose to walk the path of humility with the Lord Jesus. He pondered the humility of God expressed in the Word made flesh, a love that had to share everything with its creation, even pain and death. Following the Lord's teachings on the virtues of humility and meekness, he entered into a clearer vision of who he really was and what God meant to him. Saint Gabriel had found dignity of self, deeper repentance for failure, and the security of resurrection glory and power.

Opening Prayer

Lord, my heart is not exalted, nor are my eyes lofty. Neither have I walked in great matters, nor in wonderful things above me. If I was not humbly minded, but exalted my soul: as a child that is weaned is toward his mother, so reward in my soul. Let Israel hope in the Lord, from henceforth now and forever.

(Psalm 130)

Confrater Gabriel obediently participated in all the traditional "externals" of monasticism which aim to foster a humble monk: prostrating on the ground, begging forgiveness of the community for a wrong done, being ordered to eat sitting on the floor, and obeying various humiliating and irrational commands–the "props," so to speak, of a spirituality of his day that really were tests to prove a man's capacity to endure sufferings and humiliations to help them emulate the Suffering Servant, Jesus, and to

imitate the Lord's own self-emptying for the salvation of others.

Gabriel succeeded in fulfilling all these outward signs of humility, which was no small feat for the former leader of the self-absorbed members of the prestigious club, the "Lords of Spoleto"! Things were very different now; he was careful to take the least place of honor and attention at a gathering, known to apologize immediately after an unintentional hurt he may have caused a companion, and was silent about his many past achievements and family background. Gabriel humbly welcomed and served the strangers and the poor at the monastery door and made them feel at home. Putting his personal wants aside he became available to the person in need. He constantly took to heart the writings of the Passionist founder: "Remember that one grain of pride is sufficient to overthrow a mountain of holiness. God reveals his sublime secrets only to those who are humble of heart." (Poage, *Son of the Passion*, p.60)

In the midst of these Passionist customs of forming the virtue of humility, which everybody was obliged to practice, an internal spiritual revolution in Gabriel was gradually moving him beyond valid external aids; the emphasis was no longer on what he himself was spiritually achieving but on God's power to transform him. With each passing day, he delved deeper into the mysticism of humility, which is the very truth of who we really are before God.

Certainly, Saint Gabriel had thrown himself into the battlefield in a war against pride and a fight for the truth! The more humbly Gabriel walked before God, the clearer was his self-image of his reality–his gifts, graces, sins and faults. Preparing a sermon about the Sorrows of Mary, Gabriel penned in the margin of the rough draft a note to himself: "Remember that of myself I can't do it." (Burke, p.110) This is true humility, "a loving recognition of our total dependence on God. Moreover, Gabriel glimpsed into the truth of the other side of the coin–God's unfathomable magnificence and the faithful love he showers upon his children. As a result, an increase of awe, reverence, and gratitude engulfed Gabriel. A seeming contradiction took place but one that was in fact, harmonious because it responded to the truth of things: Gabriel experienced both his unworthiness and a need to repent for human frailty"–and also a serene confidence in the Lord's love, carrying him with courage and hope.

Consideration
No man can attain to the knowledge of God but by humility.
The way to mount high is to descend.
(Blessed Giles of Assisi)

Pause for Reflection
(Blessed Pope John XXIII, a devotee of Saint Gabriel Possenti)

"The course of my life over these last two years–28 October, 1958-59-60 –shows a spontaneous and whole-hearted intensification of union with Christ, with the Church, and with the heaven which awaits me.

I consider it a sign of great mercy shown me by the Lord Jesus that He continues to give me His peace and even exterior signs of grace which, I am told, explain the imperturbable serenity that enables me to enjoy, in every hour of my day, a simplicity and meekness of soul that keep me ready to leave all at a moment's notice and depart for eternal life.

My failings, incapacities, countless sins, offenses, and negligences for which I offer my daily Mass are causes of constant interior mortification. This prevents me from indulging in any kind of self glorification but does not weaken my confidence and trust in God, whose caressing hand I feel upon me, sustaining and encouraging.

…At the beginning of my eightieth year it is all-important for me to humble myself and lose myself in the Lord, trusting that in His mercy He will open for me the gate to eternal life. 'Jesus, Mary, Joseph, may I breathe forth my soul in peace with You.' "*

(Blessed Pope John XXIII, *Journal of a Soul*, p. 301)
This is the last part of Pope John's often used short prayer to the Holy Family; it was also the same words spoken by Saint Gabriel Possenti before his own death.

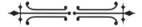

Gabriel's understanding of his servitude before the Creator stripped him of false masks and delusions about himself but did not "humiliate" or break down his dignity as a person and as a child of God! Rather, his humility permitted him the necessary attitudes to perceive the security of being loved by Love itself; it allowed Gabriel the emotional and mental freedom to be even more humble and hospitable with others, rejoicing in their successes and empathizing in their sorrows. Fulfilled himself, he could make room to listen to others and reach out to love them. So great became the interior confirmation of all he was by God's grace within him that he could let go of the need to control and possess and rest in God's Divine Providential care.

Eventually, Gabriel would be asked to lose everything that seemed good to him, even ordination to the priesthood. When the blow fiercely struck as a terminal illness, Gabriel humbly trusted the Father like a small child in his parent's arms. Some years before this ultimate sacrifice would be demanded of him, Gabriel had already written about the ironic twist of certain glory that comes from gospel humility:

"The secret of all religious success lies in the conviction that we are but dust, and that God alone can raise us up from the dust and sustain our efforts. In acknowledging oneself to be a fool, one becomes wise with the wisdom of God and is elevated to a throne of spiritual power." (Camillus, *Saint Gabriel, Passionist*, p. 88)

The Word of God
Come to me, all you who labor and are burdened, and I will give you rest. Take My yoke upon you and learn from Me, for I am meek and humble of heart; and you will find rest for your souls. For My yoke is sweet, and My burden light.

(Matthew 11: 28-30)

Closing Prayer
For let this mind be in you, which was also in Christ Jesus: Who being in the form of God, thought it not robbery to be equal to God: but emptied Himself, taking the form of a servant, being made in the likeness of men, and in habit found as a man. He humbled Himself, becoming obedient unto death, even to the death of the cross. For which cause God also has exalted Him, and has given Him a Name which is above all names: that at the Name of Jesus every knee should bow of those that are in Heaven, on earth, and under the earth: and every tongue should confess that the Lord Jesus Christ is in the glory of God the Father.

(Phil. 2:5-11)

For Further Reflection
Discovering One's True Self in God

+ Discuss with others the differences between healthy humility in one's self-understanding (a virtue) versus a humiliation that can develop into a situation of destructive behavior on one's own part or by the act of another. When are we obliged to flee the latter and seek help and refuge? On the other hand, according to Scripture, when is an insult or misunderstanding a blessing to receive, and may even be an opportunity for personal growth?

+ Prayerfully read Saint Therese's Story of a Soul, a spiritual classic on meekness, humility, creativity, and following Jesus through her "Little Way."

+ Consider the intimate connection between the humility of Jesus and His mandate for His followers to become "poor in spirit."

+ Sing/pray the beautiful Magnificat of Mary; she humbly acknowledges all her gifts and praises God, the ultimate Gift-Giver.

+ Kneel quietly before a crucifix and ponder God's humility and His extreme love for us.

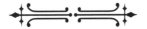

Chapter Eight

Advocate For the Poor

Gabriel, named after the great patriarch of Assisi, Saint Francis and christened "Francis" by his parents, seems to have inherited the spirit of his first patron, especially the "love of Christ's poor." (Hage, *Venerable Gabriel of Our Lady of Sorrows*, p. 224) Gabriel's biblical compassion for God's beloved poor ones began in childhood, and intensified as a Passionist; it can be said that it was the sterling charism of his entire life.

Opening Prayer
Lord, our God, for love of us, Your beloved Son accepted a crown of thorns and stood silent in the midst of insults. Teach us to recognize the face of Christ in all who suffer in body or mind. Give us strength to help them that we may daily grow in Your love. We ask this through our Lord Jesus Christ, Your Son, Who lives and reigns with You and the Holy Spirit, one God, forever and ever. Amen.
(*Votive Offices of the Passion, III. "Jesus is Crowned with Thorns,"*
Passionist Proper Offices, p.237).

Many times, the child Francis Possenti, was reprimanded by his father and governess for running out to the beggars in the street with more than ample food supplies from the family kitchen. According to their thinking, he was going too far! At times, Francis would spend his allowance to assist a poor person. (Carey, *Boy in a Hurry*, p.13) The generous child prayed daily before his favorite statue of the Pieta–the poor, naked Jesus in his

AT THE CROSS WITH MARY

mother's arms; the Holy Spirit seems to have used this humble image as an aid for Gabriel to receive the gift for a continual love of God's poor.

As a Passionist religious, this youthful enthusiasm for helping the poor greatly increased in Confrater Gabriel of the Sorrowful Virgin. He saw Christ's face in every poor person. Gabriel was not satisfied in becoming only poor *in spirit*, (Matt. 5:3), but he actually became poor, (Luke 6:20) identifying with the less fortunate, the oppressed, the abused, and the hungry. If he was to preach to the poor, he would also make himself one of them! The poverty of Jesus and Mary urged him to stretch his resources to be a beacon of God's caring to the little, the forgotten, the homeless.

Gabriel created a Sign of the Passion in the workshop. It turned out to be exceptionally beautiful; he insisted that another monk keep it instead of wearing it himself. (Hage, *Venerable Gabriel of Our Lady of Sorrows*, pp. 111-112) He also wanted the least attractive habits in the tailor shop. Gabriel would pick an old one and simply sew on patches. At meals, he eagerly followed the Passionist tradition of leaving some food aside for the poor who came to the monastery for help. Generously, he put aside the most palatable pieces of food on his plate. Often he would refrain from fruit, a favorite of his. When Gabriel gave anything, it was never the scraps! Gabriel told his companions: "Why should we leave them only the worst?" (Poage, *Son of the Passion*, p.109)

Father Godfrey Poage, C.P., remarks that Gabriel's compassion and mercy reflected God's own (Ibid.); various episodes witnessed by Gabriel's confreres illustrate this. When a poor man came to the monastery's kitchen door for food, he met the brother in charge of provisions, who was not particularly known for his magnanimity. Fortunately for the beggar, Confrater Gabriel happened to be there, most likely cleaning the dishes. Half-jokingly, Gabriel said to his Passionist brother, "I want to see your generosity this time." When the stingy monk displayed the meager portion he had cut, Gabriel seriously and unabashedly complained on behalf of the hungry person: "Poor man! Why that bit is not enough to reach his stomach!" (Norberto di S. Maria, *Vita e Virtu di S. Gabriele dell' Addolorata*, p.93) How sadly we Westerners of today and the world at large contrast to Gabriel's identification with the poor and crucified Jesus. We do not have to be "religious" to see how far society is heading into a spiraling pattern of obsessive greed and frantic materialism. Saint Gabriel is a radical, a needed sign to us today to get "in sync" with our values and holy tradition of poverty of spirit and unity with the Gospel message of Jesus.

On meditation walks or country hikes, if Gabriel had nothing material to give the poor, he would feed them with the Word of the Gospel, giving them, Father Norbert wrote, "the bread of inspiration and strength to go on." (*Norberto di Santa Maria*, p.92) Father Norbert, who knew Gabriel so well, gives invaluable insight when he describes the student as having "a predilection toward the poor". Gabriel "looked upon" the poor and prayed for them with honest love and compassion. He yearned to help them physically and spiritually. (Ibid.)

Consideration

"And so I say to the young: open your hearts to the love of God which he will give you. He loves you with tenderness. And he will give you not to keep but to share. The less you have the more you can give, and the more you have the less you can give."

(Blessed Mother Teresa of Calcutta, *Mary, Mother of Reconciliations*, p.11)

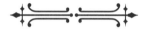

Pause for Reflection

"Father dear ... I want to say first of all that in time of scarcity and hardships God will not fail to make the most ample provision for him in the person of the poor.

"Father dear, if it were not proved by experience it would seem to be a paradox, even tempting God. What! Give all you have to the poor and then to ask God to work a miracle so that you should want for nothing? But this is more than imprudence–this is folly! That is what a badly instructed Christian might say, but he would be mistaken...

"Listen to what God says by his prophet: *Blessed is he who understands concerning the needy and the poor; the Lord will liberate him in the evil day. The Lord will preserve him and give him life and* (note this well) *make him blessed upon the earth and deliver him not up to the will of his enemies. The Lord will help him on his bed of sorrows.* (Psalm 41:1-3) This is the literal translation taken from Scripture.

"This is the remedy that frees from evil, that makes a man happy on earth and safe from his enemies, that consoles him on his death-bed. Be generous with the poor and don't be satisfied with fearfully giving them a

look of pity and only a small piece of bread...May Jesus, Mary and Joseph make you happy in time and in eternity."
(Saint Gabriel Possenti, *Letters*, from Burke, *Happy Was My Youth*, pp.226-227)

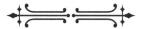

Gabriel's efforts to touch the poor in his own neighborhood were not enough according to his firm belief in the Gospel of Jesus. His sensitive awareness of the poor's plight and misery had to be told to those more fortunate. He did so by writing copious letters on the topic to his wealthy family members, making references to the poor, even urgent requests on their behalf, especially when war intensified for Italy's unification and provisions became low: "Dearest Father, be generous with the servants and specially kind to the poor...Don't be afraid, Father dear, for the giving of alms has never reduced anyone to beggary ... Jesus Christ himself has said *As often as you did it for the poor, you did it for Me....* " Gabriel also wrote to his father, "I recommend the poor to you, reminding you that I too am poor and therefore possess nothing of my own ... and yet I want for nothing, and have every convenience." (Burke, pp.152; 191)

Gabriel set down his ideals for a Passionist religious on paper, and as usual, resolutions he was determined to live: "We profess to be poor, and therefore we should act like poor men, otherwise our poverty is only make-believe and pretense." (Burke, p.190) The young cleric was already living out a radical response to the "cry of the poor."

How can we turn away from the cry of the poor when Jesus is so vi-brantly present in their sufferings? Or from the rich and haughty who may be spiritually impoverished? They have not known the depth of Jesus' love or, perhaps, have compromised what His Gospel teaches—these "wealthy" ones are truly "poor" beyond measure—spiritually speaking. We need to respond to all kinds of poverty—for God wants to be the Saviour of all! Gabriel sets a stunning example before us of concern for all the burdened and poor, according to his dear friend and spiritual director, Father Norbert, who wrote: "Sometimes, in the midst of our walks, while we were taking a rest on the road, if a poor beggar happened to pass by, Gabriel would ask permission to speak to him. He took advantage of such opportunities to instruct the poor to bear the burden of their poverty. He would encourage a filial devotion to the Madonna; he would remind them that the Son of God chose to be poor Himself, and to submit to all the inconveniences of poverty. He urged them to be mindful of the Passion of Jesus, and he spoke to them of the great reward awaiting the blessed poor in Heaven. Having thus comforted them and heartened them, he sent along their way these unfortunates whose souls, perhaps, were more famished than their bodies."

The Word of God

Is not this rather the fast that I have chosen? Loose the bands of wickedness, undo the bundles that oppress, let them that are broken go free, and break asunder every burden. Deal thy bread to the hungry and bring the needy and harborless into thy house: when thou shalt see one naked, cover him, and despise not thine own flesh. Then shall thy light break forth as the morning, and thy health shall speedily arise, and thy justice shall go before thy face, and the glory of the Lord shall gather thee up. Then shalt thou call and the Lord shall hear: Thou shalt cry and He shall say: Here I am. If thou wilt take away the chain out of the midst of thee, and cease to stretch out the finger, and to speak that which profiteth not. When thou shalt pour out thy soul to the hungry, and shalt satisfy the afflicted soul, then shall thy light rise up in darkness, and thy darkness shall be as the noonday. And the Lord will give thee rest continually, and will fill thy soul with brightness, and deliver thy bones, and thou shalt be like a watered garden, and like a fountain of water whose waters shall not fail. And the places that have been desolate for ages shall be built in thee: Thou shalt raise up the foundations of generation and generation: and thou shalt be called the repairer of fences, turning the paths into rest.

(Isaias 58:6-12)

Closing Prayer

Majestic Lady, Mother of the Poor, let me discover both the open and hidden suffering of the poor, let me see their small and comfortless dwellings, let me experience their hunger and their manifold needs, let me have sympathy for the humiliations which must be born in silence, for the contempt, embarrassment, and shame...

Open my eyes to their weariness and the burden of their material cares, to the pain which they must bear without a word of consolation.

Above all, let me recognize your poverty in theirs, and in the lines of their faces and yours, my Mother, the furrows of your Son's Countenance– He Who became poor for us! Amen.

(Adapted by Schweska from Kelly, S.J., *Youth Before God*, p.344)

For Further Reflection
Learning the Poverty of Christ

+ The first name chosen by Saint Paul of the Cross for his new congregation, the Passionists, was "The Poor of Jesus." This spirit of concrete divesting of one's unnecessary possessions, as well as the deeper emptying of one's interior life of worldly greed, lust, and self-will, is an essential to living in the spirit of the Passion of Jesus, Who stripped Himself of His glory and gave everything to the Father in naked abandonment and trust. Likewise, the poor Jesus of Bethlehem, Nazareth, and Calvary gave His all to us, in total love. Gabriel had captured this Passionist charism of being poor in possessing, but rich in giving to God and others! In our own lives of Gospel imitation, how can we practically divest ourselves of excessive possessions or the constant need to have and possess more? How can we replace the "too much" in our lives with "more room" for prayer time with God, and service projects for others in need of help and compassion?

+ Select a day of prayer and fasting in union with the poor. Entrust the homeless, poverty-stricken, and the hungry of the world to Him. If possible, give a monetary gift in connection with your day of prayer to a worthy organization that serves the poor and needy.

+ Volunteer for a soup kitchen, clothing drive, a crisis mobile, or a committee in your parish to address helping certain parishioners. Ask Saint Gabriel to guide you in this work for God and His people and to always keep your ministry to the poor as a spiritual union with Jesus, Who lives in the nakedness and the hurting of the poor.

+ Remember the spiritually poverty-stricken who are lost in their greed and have turned away from God's centrality in their lives. Be a missionary of God's gentle love to them. Prayer does change hearts. Believe in the power of prayer and your good example.

+ Ask Our Lady, Mother of the Poor, for ongoing guidance in your own unique response to the cry of the poor.

You are the light of the world. A city seated on a mountain cannot be hidden. Neither do men light a candle and put it under a bushel, but upon a candlestick, that it may shine to all that are in the house. So let your light shine before men that they may see your good works and glorify your Father in Heaven. (Matt. 5:14-16)

Chapter Nine

Ministry of Reconciliation

For if, when we were enemies, we were reconciled to God by the death of His Son; much more, being reconciled, shall we be saved by His life. (Romans 5:10) Saint Gabriel was an ambassador of God's reconciling love, making the peace of Christ his attitude and work.

Opening Prayer
"Virgin most compassionate, when thou didst fill the soul of Anna the prophetess with light, by means of thy Divine Son, thou didst make her magnify the mercies of God by recognizing Jesus as the Redeemer of the world; enrich our spirits too with heavenly grace, that we may joyfully reap in full measure the fruits of Our Lord's Redemption."
(The Raccolta, excerpt from *Novena for the Purification*)

After Gabriel hugged Sante goodbye, his earthly father, on that fateful September 6, Gabriel never saw him again. With excuses of business or illness, Sante stayed away from Gabriel. Interestingly, Gabriel's father did keep up almost a fretful correspondence with his son's superiors inquiring about his health and disposition. At the same time, the judge sent various representatives to tell Gabriel to simply return home to Spoleto.

Were Sante's excuses valid enough to keep him away for nearly six years from the son he loved so deeply and favored? Was it a subtle, cold war because Sante did not get his way? Was it a way of control or an expression of harbored feelings of disapproval? After all, we already know the manner in which Sante tried to manipulate events by hiding the Passionists' letter of acceptance of Gabriel to the novitiate. Passionist Father Jude Mead describes this incident on Sante's part as a "reprehensible action." (*Saint Gabriel, Passionist, A Youthful Gospel Portrait*, p. 56)

Today's psychological emphasis for parents to confirm their children's goals and aspirations–ultimately desiring what will really make their offspring happy and fulfilled–did not seem to be part of the thinking of Gabriel's father. Yet Gabriel continues to write respectful, loving letters to him, expressing his love and even gratitude for all the benefits he received from his father. (Ibid. p. 57) It must have taken enormous self-assurance in Gabriel's own inner being and in the call he fully embraced in order to stand firm and charitable in the face of so much strident opposition and disapproval. Gabriel's centrality of life in God the Father's love empowered him to be true to himself and to withstand the intended family pressure and projected guilt.

Nonetheless, his relationship with the Heart of Jesus and its merciful love stretched Gabriel's heart to be reconciled with Sante. Without giving in to him, Gabriel continued to remarkably and unconditionally love his father and it appears, even tried to understand whatever good intentions lay behind the man's seemingly selfish agenda. The far-reaching ramifications of Gabriel's reconciling love for his father is marvelously shown in a recent biography of the saint. Nine years after Gabriel's death, (twenty years before the formal process for his canonization was opened), his father was gravely ill with an apoplectic attack. Gabriel's brother, Father Henry Possenti, a diocesan priest, took the black and white sketch of the crucified Jesus and the Mother of Sorrows which Gabriel had held in his hands at the hour of death. He touched the ailing old Sante with the picture once so prized by his son, and Sante was instantly restored to health! Father Norbert was always convinced that this was the first, although unofficial, true miracle worked by Gabriel–and it was on behalf of his beloved father. (Cingolani, *Saint Gabriel Possenti, Passionist, A Young Man in Love*, p.153) Passionist Father Gabriele Cingolani shows us that this miracle points to an even deeper Gospel-like miracle: Gabriel's love proves to be not only forgiving and reconciling, but also undying! (Ibid.)

Gabriel was not the only family member who locked horns with the aging father and strong-willed judge. There were obviously problematic dynamics involved in the family at large and perhaps even with the servants who were like the Possenti's extended family. One of Gabriel's Christmas letters to his father reveals the lack of household harmony. As a conscientious Christian, aware of the gift of unity won for humanity by the pain of Jesus' Cross, Gabriel preaches peace in his correspondence: "...I make bold to ask you for a Christmas present this year...not as a gift for myself...but as a gift for Jesus Christ ... The gift I ask is this: unity amongst yourselves, unity in the household. Put aside all quarrels, all bitterness; forget all past injuries; preserve peace, unity, fraternal charity." (Burke, *Happy Was My Youth*, p. 146)

Gabriel's plea for peace went further than his Spoletan home; he was able to tenderly soothe others in his Passionist family who were disturbed by chaos, fear, and the ideological confusion about the war for Italy's unification. The war brought bloodshed and the terror of brigands. In spite of the seminarians' transfer to the highest plateau of the Apennines, (a decision made out of concern for their safety) the warring factions found their way even to the small, remote town of Isola. Rebels for unity were everywhere. Mixed with these patriots were ruffians who sought only to loot and plunder. Isola, situated in the Kingdom of Naples at that time, was warned by the government not to aid the opposing forces in any way.

However, little choice was left to the monks; the revolutionary band easily ran through the monastery and took what food and supplies they wanted. This pandemonium was followed by the royal guard's invasion of the cloister and their hot pursuit of the enemy. "They searched the retreat and scoured the grounds for fugitives." (Ibid, p.207) Gabriel remained a bulwark of strength to his worried superiors and companions at this time, advocating instead peaceful attitudes in the spirit of Jesus and asking others to trust in God relating to their own personal protection. "God is thinking of us! Nothing can happen to us except by God's will!" (Ibid, p.208)

Most of the religious obviously sided with the Church's position to preserve the Papal States, contrary to the vast, general movement for one, united Italy. Gabriel was among the former for sure, but his personal political stance didn't cloud his view of himself as a Christian monk; above all positions and arguments, he saw himself as an official *pray-er* of the Church, a professed man of prayer–prayer that was meant to create a neutral bridge for all the children of God to find the peace and forgiveness of Christ. He refused to hate even the so-called enemies of the pope. Gabriel wrote home: "The men who are the originators of this dreadful state of affairs should be regarded as the instruments in the hand of God to try the fidelity of the good and to punish the sins of the wicked and to purify the Church. Regarding these enemies of law and order and the Church, we should not entertain any bitterness nor the desire of revenge. We ought rather to commiserate them, while we pray with the Church: 'That Thou wouldst deign to humble the enemies of the Church.' " (Poage, p.110) It was a courageous position to take, one that seems to emerge only after painful and honest prayer over the double-edged sword of Christ's Gospel.

Consideration

Have you ever experienced the utter exhilaration of "letting go" of a grudge or hurt–and just forgiving someone with no strings attached? Those who dare to cross this miraculous boundary are like explorers who discover a new domain; ultimately, only God can bring them there, and yet, only with their permission.

Pause for Reflection

If then any man is in Christ, he is a new creature: the former things have passed away; behold they are made new! But all things are from God, Who has reconciled us to Himself through Christ and has given to us the ministry of reconciliation.

(II Corinthians 5: 17-21)

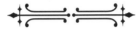

I remember one day in the late 60's in elementary school the class was studying the religious bulletin we received monthly; it was a well-done fold-out with current events, illustrated sketches of interesting saints, and a scripture study box. That particular day we read Saint Paul's letter about reconciliation and being Christ's ambassadors. An ambassador conjured up images for me of the United Nations and peace talks! I took the concept to heart. I wanted to be the distinguished ambassador of Christ!

Later, in high school, I realized that sticking to one's convictions about principles in the gospel and turning the other cheek for Christ rarely got me any admiration from my peers. It meant certain times of being alone and feeling left out. Fortunately, I met up with teenagers in the CYO (Christian Youth Organization) who shared my Catholic views and helped me grow in my faith by our solidarity in Christ. We learned by shared experiences, that while striving and praying for the ideal peace and fraternal bond we wanted, we would have to encounter unavoidable opposition and even ridicule for the sake of Jesus. Our relationship with Christ needed to be our sustaining grace. Being an ambassador no longer meant a glamorized position for myself; rather, it became a natural consequence of loving Christ and wanting to re-present him to the world.

Ambassadors have a very difficult job; they seek the ultimate result of peace but not by compromising human dignity or the integrity of the truth. Saint Gabriel was an ambassador for Christ and His reconciling love.

He, too, learned how paradoxical the Lord's peace can be! While loving his father as much as he was able to in reconciling letters, Gabriel refused to turn back on his Passionist vocation–a religious life that terribly displeased his father. Gabriel would not be untrue to himself! It is doubtful if Gabriel's position of reconciliation was ever truly acceptable on his father's part. Listening to the Gospel, Gabriel's vision broadened wide

enough to allow him to see the good benefits he had received from his father, his father's virtues, and the possible and even understandable motives regarding his father's inability to bless Gabriel's lifestyle.

Gabriel went even further; remaining loyal to the Church and his own political stance, he also wanted to understand the motives and sufferings of the revolutionists. Gabriel reflected that the war might be a possible and positive time of purification for the Church in the midst of havoc and destruction. Meanwhile, he faithfully prayed for God's victory to uphold the Church and deliver it from harm. What a remarkable balance and what courage it takes to stand in the middle! Often we find the courage and strength in the middle with God and our heavenly friends on either side of us to eventually make ultimate and radical choices when and if the time presents itself—as the martyrs, both of olden days and modern times, know so well!

Seeking the peace of Jesus has many angles and cannot be simplified. Jesus' peace compels each of us to be true to our deepest expression of self and to the God of radical loving who calls us to Himself. Isaias reminds us that God's ways are not always our ways (55:8); we shouldn't be surprised when Jesus' own kind of peace does not make everyone happy. On the contrary!! Jesus warned us of the terrible obstacles we will encounter as we struggle for unity.

The Cross Christ endured will never let us forget the price of reconciliation. The cross we may have to carry in the name of peace may strangely demand an unavoidable, painful division with loved ones which has to take place before God's grace can bring all those involved into a visible conciliation. Forgiving those who abused or betrayed us will always be a miraculous event and only God's Spirit can aid us. Constantly examining our motives and our consciences in the light of Jesus' truth, we are called to pray again and again for a more perfect peace to take place in our lives and in the world. Unity is always the goal. When our efforts are weak and even futile, we need to re-commit our lives to the Lord's burning desire: *May they all be one.* (John 17:21) The world is broken, but the potential of Christ's healing love can heal others and fill the voids in their lives. As His agents, His very ambassadors, we set ourselves to the task of peace making. It will be frustrating work but rewarding. We may build one bridge and, at the same time, see another fall down. At times, we can surprisingly experience both the drive to love and forget injuries against us and also still harbor anger and resentment toward those who seem to antagonize us or thwart our peaceful approach to them.

Saint Gabriel's great love for the Sacrament of Confession helped him find unity within himself first and then to build upon the special grace received through it. He often sought out Father Norbert for confession, realizing his own need for God's forgiveness. Someone who is not forgiven in the inner sanctum of his or her person can never extend the reign of Christ's peace. Ultimately, we hope and believe that Christ will put all things under His domain of love, once and for all. For now, we trust in His grace to do our part. Unity with God and one another is the gift of the saving Cross. In baptism, like Saint Gabriel and all the saints who strove to live lives of peace and reconciliation, we are sealed with the cross, and bonded as one family in Jesus' blood. Penance and the Sacrament of Confession cleanse us anew in Christ's healing Blood. This Precious Blood is the life force that will guide our peaceful steps ...*Through Him He should reconcile to*

Himself all things, whether on the earth or in the heavens, making peace through the blood of His cross. (Colossians 1:20)

The Word of God

And when they were come to the place which is called Calvary, they crucified Him there; and the robbers, one on the right hand and the other on the left. And Jesus said, "Father, forgive them, for they know not what they do." But they, dividing His garments, cast lots. And the people stood beholding, and the rulers with them derided Him saying, "He saved others, let Him save Himself, if He be the Christ, the elect of God"....And one of the robbers who was hanged blasphemed Him saying, "If You are the Christ save Yourself and us." But the other answering, rebuked him saying, "Neither do you fear God, seeing that you are under the same condemnation? And we indeed justly for we receive the due reward of our deeds; but this man has done no evil." And he said to Jesus, "Lord, remember me when You shall come into Your Kingdom." And Jesus said to him, "Amen, I say to you: This day you shall be with Me in Paradise."

(Luke 23: 33-35; 39-43)

Closing Prayer

Father, all-powerful and ever-living God, we praise and thank You through Jesus Christ our Lord for Your presence and action in the world. In the midst of conflict and division, we know it is You Who turn our minds to thoughts of peace. Your Spirit changes our hearts: enemies begin to speak to one another, those who were estranged join hands in friendship, and nations seek the way of peace together. Your Spirit is at work when understanding puts an end to strife, when hatred is quenched by mercy, and vengeance gives way to forgiveness. For this we never cease to thank and praise You. We join with all the choirs of Heaven as they sing forever to Your glory: Holy, Holy, Holy...

(Preface, The Roman Missal, 1985.)

For Further Reflection
Living Christ's Peace

+ Discuss in a small group the pains and struggles in courageously following your own path of truth instead of the way of someone you care about but who does not believe in your dreams, ideals, or the goals you set for yourself. How do you maintain peace? Is it always possible?

+ In your imagination think of the gentle, forgiving Heart of Jesus. He is your Friend and Redeemer. Bask in that light and friendship. Now, envision next to Jesus someone you know who is impossible for you to deal with, or who has injured you in some way. See that person you dislike being transformed by the warm, healing rays from the Heart of Christ. Picture the Lord reaching out with His arm to this person, enfolding him in His embrace. Pray for this person.

+ Say a Rosary—quietly, slowly, thinking of the nations of the world, especially those torn apart by terrorism, injustice, poverty, and war. Ask Mary, Queen of Peace, to bring her Son's healing to them and His enlightenment to their transgressors. Pray, too, for true justice for all those involved.

+ In your own words to Christ or with a companion on a walk, talk out the relationships with your family or friends that are troubling you, and need God's reconciling love. Consider how you yourself can become a catalyst in this healing process.

+ Jesus demonstrated what the Church calls "righteous anger" in several Gospel situations. We must see this side of Christ in the very midst of His ultimate mission of peace and reconciliation. Discuss in groups and share insights about this Gospel element.

+ Jesus challenges us to pray for the wisdom to recognize our own course of action—always depending on Him to guide us and purify our motives. This requires much prayer.

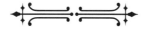

Chapter Ten

Blessed Friendships and Spiritual Guides

Gabriel had a penchant for friendships that were honest, wholesome, and spiritually creative. He opened up his heart to special companions, above all to Father Norbert, his spiritual director. These friendships became a mutual source of grace and were a reflection of the guiding presence and faithful love of God in their lives.

Opening Prayer
*"O Jesus...it seems to me that you cannot fill a soul with more love than
the love with which You have filled mine; ... I dare to ask You to love
those whom you have given me with the love with which You loved me."*
(O'Conner, *In Search of Therese*, p.100)

Saint Ignatius of Antioch's advice concerning friendship given in the early days of the Church would find an echo in the heart of Gabriel, who resolved to be friendly and helpful to all, especially the least-liked in the monastery: "Let none of you take a merely natural attitude toward his neighbor but love one another continually in Christ Jesus." However he also had special, unique friends he cared about and who were soul-mates, sharing the path of faith with him.

When Gabriel left Spoleto for the Passionists, his closest boyhood and college friend, Philip Giovannetti attended law school, and although they live in two separate worlds, they communicated. Gabriel's sincerity and warmth comes through in a long letter he wrote to Philip regarding the need to keep a spiritual life as a law student, and to avoid whatever might destroy Philip's relationship with Christ. Also, in response to Philip's request for a useful prayer book, Gabriel was only too happy to comply, mailing it to him at once. (Cavatassi & Giorgini, Eds., *Fonti/Storico-Biografiche*, pp.323-325) It was his usual, caring way toward people–outreaching, showing genuine concern for the spiritual well-being of a friend, and thoughtful to the last detail.

Venerable Father Norbert

Another beautiful image of friendship in Gabriel's life is Francis Dionisi, a medical student, whose uncle was the parish priest of Isola; he spoke with Gabriel whenever he had a chance to do so. Gabriel's views on the deeper realities of life were an impressive factor in the future doctor's development as a person and professional. In turn, Francis was a support to Gabriel in 1861-62 when Gabriel shared with him the news that he was dying of tuberculosis. Gabriel spoke with some pathos about his oncoming death; and yet he also revealed a tremendous hope in the life to come, a conviction that the medical student would always remember, later testifying to it in the process of canonization. (Ibid, pp.418-420)

Standing out beyond all the images of Gabriel's friendships was a spirit-blessed one, his spiritual director and guide, Father Norbert Cassinelli of Saint Mary. Eleven years older than Gabriel, Father Norbert writes, "I first met Confrater Gabriel on the day he entered the novitiate at Morravalle, and from that moment we were never separated ... I was entrusted with all the secrets of his heart ... He committed his whole soul into my hands: his thoughts, his desires, his repugnances ... In the manifestation of his heart, he acted with a simplicity and candor worthy of imitation." (Farnum, *Saint Gabriel*, p. 195-196.)

In Father Norbert, Gabriel had providentially been given a spiritual support, a necessary guide for the challenging vocation Gabriel had chosen. Although Gabriel would never see his own father again, Norbert would be there for Gabriel everyday of his monastic life, even at the youth's dying hour. Norbert was more than a director; he was a living sign to Gabriel that God is faithful and true until the end! In turn, Norbert's priesthood and religious life were evidently renewed.

Norbert's writings show how intensely exciting it was, on a spiritual level, to participate in the formation of a saint. The writings also reflect a man who has been touched by grace through another person placed in his life by God. In fact, Norbert's entire life after Gabriel's death was enhanced by the fact that he was to spread the story of the saintly young man. People looked upon Norbert as a blessed priest, honored by God to have directed and been associated with one of his special servants. A Passionist who interviewed Father Norbert on the day of Gabriel's beatification ceremony writes: "When the old man spoke of his beloved son, his eyes filled with tears and a beautiful smile lit up his face...The six-and-forty years since the saintly boy had died seemed but a day to his aged master, and Gabriel is always present with him." (Camillus, *Saint Gabriel, Passionist*, p. 258-262)

In a very real way then, the former director of the saint, could lovingly express to Gabriel as Saint Paul did to his spiritual son, Timothy, *I remember you constantly in my prayers, night and day... I yearn to see you again...* (II Tim.1: 3-4) After the beatification ceremony, Pope Saint Pius X came over to meet with Norbert and to bless him. Then, two Passionist brothers escorted Norbert as they left Saint Peter's in the grand recessional. People tried to get a glimpse of or touch the holy man who had been so close to the new *Beato*. The same Passionist who had spoken with Norbert earlier that day observed, "And as I watched him, I felt that so must the aged Simeon have looked as he left the temple of old, singing his *Nunc Dimittis*." (Ibid, pp. 263-264)

Consideration

"I can never lose one whom I have loved unto the end; one to whom my soul cleaves so firmly that it can never be separated... Be mindful of me when you come to where I shall follow."

(Saint Bernard)

Pause for Reflection

If there be any consolation in Christ, if any comfort in charity, if any society of the spirit, if any depths of commiseration: fulfill my joy, that you be of one mind, having the same charity, being of one accord, agreeing in sentiment. Let nothing be done through contention, neither by vain glory, but in humility, let each esteem others better than himself, each one not considering the things that are his own, but those that are other men's.

(Philippians 2:1-4)

Gabriel and Norbert empowered each other to become saints. (Father Norbert of Saint Mary died June 29, 1911, and was made "Venerable" by Pope John Paul II on December 15, 1994.) In spite of the formal framework of spiritual direction, an intimate friendship unexpectedly and necessarily developed between Gabriel and Norbert. Gabriel could not have possibly revealed the totality of his heart and soul, as he did, for nearly six years and not experience a valid, trusting friendship with his superior.

Jesus describes friendship as the very sharing of one's intimate inner self, especially when it concerns the Spirit at work within us. (John 15:15) Norbert, on the other hand, was consistently involved in the well-being of his charge, Confrater Gabriel. His own love for his spiritual son was evident in unabashed concern and worry for the youth's health, the attention he paid in corresponding with Judge Possenti, and especially in the goodness he displayed during Gabriel's drawn-out sickness and painful death. Norbert confessed, "I was filled with sorrow at the thought of losing this dear boy and no matter how I argued the point with myself, I could not control my emotions." (Burke, *Happy Was My Youth*, p. 241)

Gabriel was also very perceptive of Norbert's feelings, completely aware of the special bond they shared. Norbert relates, "My grief did not escape his keen eye. Despite his weakness, he always tried to talk to me. He tried to hide the inevitable decline of his failing strength. He tried to make me realize the joy which filled his soul and thus to ease and comfort my own anguish." (Ibid.) After Gabriel died, Norbert participated in the funeral rites but did not stay for the actual interment. He candidly admitted to the community that in spite of his faith as a religious, he didn't have the heart to see Gabriel's body lowered into the crypt. He could not watch that heavily symbolic, final farewell. (Farnum, p.188)

Norbert was honest with his human feelings; he was much like Saints Augustine, Bernard, Aelred, and Jane Frances de Chantal–each richly imbedded in Christ and the promises of eternal life–yet freely able to express the deepest pain over the loss of their friends in death. Norbert and Gabriel's friendship was a very human love; it contained joy and, as evident in Norbert's words, some painful struggle. Their friendship, begun in spiritual direction, grew and expanded in meaning and in union with Christ Crucified who was simultaneously sanctifying both men. It was a blessed union that motivated them both to go outwards to their community and to others in the love and service of God. This holy bond between them would eventually leap out of this short time span and restricted space on earth and continue, uninterrupted in the realm of a new, indescribable and eternal life in heaven. Perhaps it was their marvelous faith-life that enabled them to see in their mutual association the very One, the Holy Christ, the Divine

Lover—Whom they mutually served and adored.

"When we are linked by the power of prayer, we as it were hold each other's hand as we walk side by side along a slippery path; and thus by the bounteous disposition of charity, it comes about that the harder each one leans on the other, the more firmly we are riveted in brotherly love."

(Saint Gregory the Great)

The Word of God

And not for them only do I pray, but for them also who through their word shall believe in Me; that they all may be one as Thou, Father, in Me and I in Thee; that they also may be one in us; that the world may believe that You have sent Me. And the glory which You have given Me, I have given them, that they may be one as we also are one. I in them, and You in Me; that they may be made perfect in one, and the world may know that You have sent Me, and has loved them as you also have loved Me. Father, I will that where I am they also, whom You have given Me, may be with Me; that they may see My glory which You have given Me, because You have loved Me before the creation of the world.... And I have made known Your Name to them, and will make it known; that the love wherewith You have loved Me, may be in them and I in them.

(John 17: 20-24; 26)

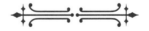

Closing Prayer

Beloved Jesus, through my faith experiences, I've come to see and believe: that "they whom God forces to part with their near of kin, for His sake, find brethren in the spirit at their side. They who remain solitary, for His sake, have children raised up to them. How should we thank God for this great benefit! He gives, He takes away; blessed be His Name. But He takes away to give again, and He withdraws one blessing to restore four-fold."

My God and my all, not only to these particular vocations are given such marvelous gifts, but "we, too, through God's mercy, whether we be young or old, whether we have friends or few, if we be Christ's, shall all along our pilgrimage find those in whom we may live, who will love us and whom we may love, who will aid us and help us forward, and comfort us, and close our eyes. For His love is a secret gift, which unseen by the world, binds together those in whom it lives, and makes them live and sympathize in one another."

(Adapted as a prayer by John J. Schweska
from the writings of Venerable Cardinal Newman.)

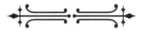

For Further Reflection
Companions for the Faith Journey

+ Discuss with others the qualities you consider of a good friendship. In what ways does such a friendship integrate into your love for God?

+ Spend half an hour before the Blessed Sacrament. Ask the Lord for a spiritual director who will understand you well and guide you in a deeper faith life of conversion and commitment. If you already have such a person, pray for continued blessings upon this relationship and its foundation to be based on mutual love for God and zeal for His Kingdom.

+ Plan a meeting with a best friend. Walk together on a nature trail—by the sea, in the woods, or up a mountain. Make preparations beforehand so that you can both rest for a while and share a packed lunch or an early dinner. Make this a sacred time; pray psalms, sing hymns, and make prayers of intercession.

+ Remember someone today who blessed your life at a particular crossing point in your spiritual journey and who made a difference for you. Write a note or phone this person to say hello.

+ If you love your friend, pray about effective ways to build up and support his/her and your own Faith life. Share with one another the love of Jesus' sacrifice on the cross—which is the most graphic sign of God's outpouring love for humanity—the bond of all friendships.

+ True Christian friends point each other to the Friend of all friends. Listen and pray over the words of Monsignor Benson from his spiritual classic, *The Friendship of Christ*: "…awaken to the fact that Christ desires more than mere obedience, mere faith, mere adoration—that he desires such a friendship with Himself that its inception is no less than a moral conversion…a soul in this manner becoming conscious—as a maiden become conscious that she is love—of the heart-shaking fact that God is her Lover."

+ *Will you lay down your life for Me?* (John 13:38)

+ *Amen, amen, I say to you, unless a grain of wheat falls to the ground and dies, it remains alone; but if it dies, it brings forth much fruit.*

(John 12:24)

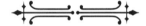

Chapter Eleven

Living in the Eucharist; Remembering the Lord's Passion

Saint Gabriel's centrality of self was in Jesus' saving Paschal Mystery. As a man of worship in spirit and truth, he gave praise to God by contemplating Christ's sacred Passion. From the light he received from the Word of the Cross, Gabriel lived his life eucharistically, united to Jesus' redeeming sacrifice.

Opening Prayer
O God, Who in this wonderful Sacrament, left us a memorial of Your Passion: grant, we implore You, that we may so worship the sacred mysteries of Your Body and Blood, as always to be conscious of the fruit of Your Redemption. You Who lives forever and ever. Amen.

University students preparing for their exams, who were recommended by the local bishop to stay a few days at the quiet of the Pievetorina Retreat, were hiking about the wooded surroundings. One of them came upon a scene that would impress him for the rest of his life. Hidden in a grove was the familiar Passionist seminarian—Confrater Gabriel. He was lost in prayer, oblivious to their discovery of his secret space. His arms were extended in the form of a cross, a custom of prayer for religious of his day. His face was aglow with joy. It was as if Gabriel was bathed in a supernatural light. He didn't seem to mind the rough stones scattered all about the ground where he knelt in perfect repose. The observer marveled at the sight of serenity and he had the sense that Gabriel was communicating with God. (Burke, *Happy Was My Youth*, pp.140-1) Gabriel appeared to be living the words of his holy founder who wrote that prayer should be like "fishing in spirit in the sea of the Passion...an ocean of love...Dive into its depth. No matter how deep you go, you will never reach bottom..." (Bialas, *In This Sign, The Spirituality of Saint Paul of the Cross*, p.75)

Gabriel's love for the Passion and Cross of Jesus was a key aspect of his identity as a Passionist religious. Father Norbert attested that Gabriel's whole life was one of contemplation of the Lord's love expressed so magnificently and totally in Jesus' sufferings, the outpouring of Christ's Precious Blood and the image of the wounded and open Sacred Heart. Gabriel was drawn daily to his crucifix, received at his profession. "For Gabriel, the crucifix became the book of life; therein he studied the mystery of a crucified God, humility, patience, and love supreme..." (Hage, *The Life of Venerable Gabriel of Our Lady of Sorrows*, p.204) His understanding of the Blood of Jesus instilled in Gabriel the desire to give as totally as the Lord gave, making his life an oblation of love in return for Christ's love. Upon careful study, it can be seen that his entire "Passion" prayer and spirituality was particularly prayed within the framework of two important spiritual

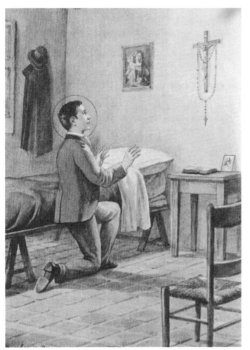

realities of the Paschal Mystery—*by* "atonement" and *in* the "Eucharist."

Gabriel offered up his entire self "in union" with the atoning Cross of his Brother, Jesus—in reparation for his own failings and for the brokenness of the world around him—praying and living for the purpose of Jesus' atonement: reconciliation with God, within Gabriel's own broken self and with all God's children and creation. Praying and living to accomplish this unity of life brought Gabriel more intimately into contact with God's life and kingdom and with Christ's health-giving unity!

Gabriel realized fully that "In all He did from the Incarnation to the Cross, the end Jesus Christ had in mind was the gift of the Eucharist, His personal, corporal union with each Christian through Communion. He saw the means of communicating to us all the treasures of His Passion, all the virtues of His Sacred Humanity, and all the merits of His life." (Saint Peter Julian Eymard)

In the celebration of the Holy Mass, Gabriel worshipped in communion with Christ and offered the sacramental renewal of Jesus' death on the altar. The Eucharistic banquet and sacrifice was for Saint Gabriel the joy of his monastic days. It gave meaning to his religious vocation and strengthened him to live his vows to God. The "Memorial of the Passion," the Blessed Sacrament was particularly important for him as a Passionist. The Gospel of John graphically describes the blood and water flowing forth from the side of Jesus after the centurion pierced the Lord's Heart. (19:34) The Fathers of the Church saw in this the birth of the Church and the Sacramental Life, particularly the Eucharist and Baptism.

Consideration
But may I never boast except in the cross of our Lord Jesus Christ, through which the world has been crucified to me, and I to the world.
(Gal. 6:14)

Pause for Reflection
"But in this we can glory: in our infirmities (cf. Cor. 12:5) and bearing daily the holy Cross of our Lord Jesus Christ (cf. Luke 14:27) ... Let all of us, brothers, look to the Good Shepherd Who suffered the Passion of the Cross to save His sheep. The sheep of the Lord followed Him in tribulation and persecution, in insult and hunger, in infirmity and temptation, and in everything else, and they have received everlasting life from the Lord because of these things."

(Saint Francis of Assisi, *"The Admonitions" from Francis and Clare*, The Complete works, translated by R. J. Armstrong, OFM CAP & I.C. Brady, O.F.M., p. 29)

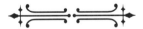

Gabriel firmly believed that his own sacrifices in monastic life and his prayers were also prayerfully surging in the Blood of Christ *through* the Church and to the universe, making a creative, healing mark. Gabriel, like the Apostle Paul, could truly say with love: *Now rejoice in my sufferings for you, and fill up those things that are wanting of the sufferings of Christ, in my flesh, for His Body, which is the Church...* (Colossians 1:24) Thereby, Gabriel's activities of praise, petition, and acts of charity for others were like currents of spiritual, healing energy which he extended to the painful events of his time, to his family and friends, and even to the

souls in Purgatory to whom he had an extraordinary devotion.

Blessed Elizabeth of the Trinity describes the sum of "all holiness" and "all apostolate" in two words: "Union and Love." (*Elizabeth of the Trinity, The Complete Works*, Vol. I, p.24) Life itself holds enough challenges to motivate us to proclaim and live for Christ, that one way or another, we shall come to know a spiritual type, but none the less real bleeding, like Jesus—for the sake of love.

In the words of Saint Philip Neri, the joyful founder of the Oratorians, "Nothing more glorious can happen to a Christian than to suffer for Christ."

Intimately bound to the Passion of Jesus and our own spiritual dying is the Eucharist itself. Gabriel acted out this precise meaning and spirit of the Eucharist throughout the entire day by how he prayed, thought and lived his faith life within his community. Visiting the Blessed Sacrament in chapel, Gabriel's source of thanksgiving was, "He who suffered and died for me is here!" (Hage, p.203). From this Presence, as from a fresh spring, Gabriel drew from the promised waters of Jesus: *He that believes in Me, as the Scripture says," Out of His belly shall flow fountains of living water."* (John 7:38) For Gabriel, as with Saint Paul of the Cross, the founder of the Passionists, the Eucharist and the Passion were "one—the revelation of God's love for us." (Bialas, C.P., *The Mysticism of the Passion in Saint Paul of the Cross*, p.189)

Gabriel's prayer, as one with Jesus' atonement on the Cross and fed by the same Lord in the Eucharist, developed Gabriel into a person who knew that his own body was to be broken as bread and given to feed hungry souls. His own blood (the striking Hebrew symbol of a person's life-force) was also poured out in his battle with tuberculosis (numerous blood sheddings through hemoptysis) and his real *desire* (a "dry" martyrdom as it is called) to help thirsting hearts—people who seek the Face of God was fulfilled! The cross was Gabriel's light in all his joys and struggles. In a letter to his father, he wrote: "Whoever does not carry the Cross of Jesus Christ and does not follow Him cannot be His disciple. You tell me you are carrying the Cross; this is a good sign, for this is what He wants of you." (Cingolani, C.P., *Life and Prayers*, p.80) In 1859, Gabriel writes in his meditations: "Jesus went to excess in order to show us His love. He could have saved us a number of ways—all it would have taken was a drop of blood, a tear, a prayer; it wasn't necessary that He die. But what would have been enough for justice was not sufficient for love." (Ibid, pp.80-1) Gabriel saw the same and related excess of love in Jesus' institution of the Eucharist!

The Word of God
For I have received of the Lord that which I also delivered unto you: that the Lord Jesus, the same night in which He was betrayed, took bread, and giving thanks, broke and said, "Take and eat: This is My Body, which shall be delivered for you. Do this for a commemoration of Me." In like manner also the chalice, after He had supped, saying, "This chalice is the new testament of My Blood. This do, as often as you shall drink, for the commemoration of Me." For as often as you shall eat this bread, and drink the chalice, you shall show the death of the Lord, until He comes.

(I Corinthians 11:23-26)

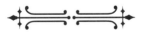

Closing Prayers
O God, according to your marvelous plan of love You called Saint Gabriel of Our Lady of Sorrows to live the mystery of the Cross. Together with Mary, the mother of Jesus, guide our spirit to your Crucified Son, so

that as sharers in His Passion and Death, we may obtain the glory of the Resurrection. We ask this through Christ our Lord. Amen.

(Cingolani, Life and Prayers, p.37)

Father, all-powerful and ever-living God, we do well always and everywhere to give You thanks through Jesus Christ, our Lord.

Lifted high on the Cross, Christ gave His life for us, so much did He love us. From His wounded side flowed blood and water, the fountain of sacramental life in the Church. To His open Heart the Savior invites all to draw water in joy from the springs of salvation.

Now with all the saints and angels, we praise You forever: Holy, holy, holy Lord! Heaven and earth are filled with Your glory, Hosanna in the highest, Blessed is He Who comes in the Name of the Lord, Hosanna in the highest!

(Preface, Mass of the Sacred Heart, Roman Sacramentary)

For Further Reflection
"In Remembrance of Me"

+ Spend fifteen minutes to an hour before the Tabernacle; bask in His Eucharistic Presence as in the warm rays of the sun. Receive His energy, His Spirit! Meditate on God's love.

+ Have lunch with a less popular person at work or school. Offer them some interesting, friendly, and congenial company. See the Lord in their loneliness; perhaps you may bring some light and peace into their lives. Maybe a surprise discovery awaits you when you discover a charm or goodness in the person you had not previously seen or appreciated.

+ Find a good book on the Paschal Mystery, the Eucharist, or the mystery of suffering in the world. Read it prayerfully, take notes or underline important passages; apply a little of what you found impressive in the reading to your day's activities.

+ Attempt to spend some quiet time in prayerful remembrance of Jesus' Passion; ponder the words of Saint Paul of the Cross: "Dive into its depths. No matter how deep you go, you will never reach the bottom..." (Bialas, C.P., *The Mysticism of the Passion in Saint Paul of the Cross*, p. 189)

+ The founders of the Franciscan Society of the Atonement, Father Paul Watson and Mother Lurana White, were inspired by the mystery of the atonement of Jesus. Within the word *atonement*, they marveled at their discovery of the word within the word: "AT-ONE-MENT"! Reflecting and praying together upon this led them to begin the week-long prayer in January for unity with the Chair of Peter among all Christians. How do the words **atonement** and **at-one-ment** fit into your life in Christ and with others as a passionate and creative desire for you?

+ "The time after Communion is the most precious time in our life; it is the fittest time for negotiating with God, and for inflaming our souls with His divine love."(Saint Mary Magdalen de Pazzi) Considering these awesome words of reflection, let us prepare our hearts and bodies worthily by earnest prayer before receiving the Body and Blood of the Living Lord.

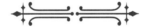

Chapter Twelve

The Presence of Mary

Gabriel walked the journey of the Spirit with Mary. By a special grace from God, Gabriel experienced the intimacy of Mary's companionship and was instructed in the school of her unique gospel insight. Mary was the feminine touchstone of Gabriel's personality, integrating the best qualities of his manhood. As the first disciple of Jesus, and particularly as faithful Mother of the crucified Lord, Mary became the prism through which Gabriel saw Christ more perceptively and the world He came to redeem.

Opening Prayer

Lord, You gave Saint Gabriel of Our Lady of Sorrows a special love for
Your mother and a compassion for her sorrows.
Through her, You raised him to the heights of holiness.
Give us great devotion to her sorrows, that we may know her
as our loving mother. We ask this through our Lord Jesus Christ. Amen.
(Prayer, *Feast of Saint Gabriel*, Passionist Proper Offices, p.78)

Servant of God, Pope John Paul II, in his encyclical, "Mother of the Redeemer," writes: "Mary is present in the Church as the Mother of Christ, and at the same time as that Mother whom Christ, in the mystery of the Redemption, gave to humanity in the person of the Apostle John. Thus, in her new motherhood in the Spirit, Mary embraces each and every one in the Church, and ... through the Church." (Article 47, p.66) The sacred memory and active presence of Mary in the life of the Church *from the*

beginning (Acts 1:1) goes beyond devotional love; it is an experience. (Laurentin, *A Year of Grace with Mary, Rediscovering the Significance of her Role in the Christian Life*, p. 115)

Saint Gabriel found this active, living, and loving relationship with a very real, concerned, and caring mother–the Virgin Mary–when he was but four years old, grieving over the death of his mother, Agnes. Through the tenderness and teachings of his sister and close friend, Maria Luisa, and the simple devotion around the statue of Our Lady of Sorrows, Mary somehow touched the child with the gift of experiencing her motherly presence. The moment this happened is a secret one as God's Spirit blows within the recesses of our souls when and as it wills. (John 3: 8)

Gabriel's early expressions of this spirit-filled event are recorded. He kept a constant vigil light burning before the little statue in his room, visited the famous churches in Spoleto, and prayed at the Marian altars which were most neglected or abandoned. He instructed his playmates, and later, his school companions to make the same visits to Mary, to have a bold confidence in her, and to never forget her. His love was poetically expressed in the flowers he picked for Mary's shrines and the language he used regarding her; it had a trace of the medieval loyalty connected to knightly love–much akin to the expression of love for God and Mary used by Saint Francis of Assisi. (De Paris, G., O.F.M. Cap., *I Know Christ*, p.32) Gabriel, too, was Mary's troubadour and the jongleur of her Son's saving wounds!

As time progressed, Gabriel's understanding of Mary as an important Gospel figure continually developed. He learned about her role in salvation history through his excellent scholastic and religious training by the Christian Brothers and the Jesuits. Gabriel explored the Bible passages relating to Mary and her relationship to Christ, and meditated on these Gospel scenes in the rosary. (Many times he was seen, after a night at the opera or a hunting expedition, stealing away to a remote place to say the daily rosary.)

As a teenager in college, Gabriel wrote a mature poem about the Virgin Mary's surrender, her *fiat* given to the angel of the Annunciation. (Ceci, *Scritti di S. Gabriele dell' Addolorata, Studente Passionista*, pp.59-66) He also wrote a lengthy poem *To The Virgin Standing Near the Cross* demonstrating his perceptive ideas about Mary's involvement with all the sorrows and needs of God's people. (Ibid, pp. 111-123).

Gabriel's companionship with Mary was a significant aid to him against the powerful temptations of his adolescence. He kept her present in his thoughts; it seems, even in the midst of his studies, parties, sports, and his restless search for happiness as a Spoletan youth. Later on in his life, he expressed that without her intercession on his behalf at this time, he would have surely lost his way or chosen the wrong path for himself.

The purity of mind, body and speech which Gabriel always preserved, even in the early days of indecision, is difficult to understand in today's sexually saturated society; we most likely relate much easier to his glamorous and fun pastimes than to his chivalrous love for purity in all things. This pure image had nothing to do with a man who had no options for different expressions of love, or of a passionless, pious individual.

Gabriel was very fond of the young lady, Maria Pennacchietti, and all accounts attest to their relationship as a budding romance, full of promise, and smiled upon by their families. The British Passionist, Father Wilson, believed that Gabriel's "sublimation of his love" for the Virgin Mary was the reason for Gospel chastity which he achieved for the sake of Christ's kingdom. (*Saint Gabriel, Student, Passionist, Saint*, p.16)

The Mother of God became a veritable tutor to Gabriel in the way of the Gospel. In 1962, Blessed Pope John XXIII wrote about Saint Gabriel's keen awareness and cooperation with Mary's spiritual work in his life: "The Virgin Mother was always present in his thoughts, in her was his refuge in the ups-and-downs of daily life; he devoutly contemplated and desired to share her sorrows; in her he habitually put all his confidence." (*Letter on the Centenary of the Death of Saint Gabriel*) With Mary, Gabriel eventually learned how to repeat her "yes" to God, making his own yes to a vocation from God–which he received through an interior voice, the voice of Mary. He actually learned how to see other people through Mary's sorrowful motherlike gaze; how else can one explain the extraordinary charism of Gabriel's life–his love for the poor? Through Mary's eyes, Gabriel loved the suffering sisters and brothers of Jesus and Mary's own spiritual children. It was Mary who helped Gabriel in "that monumental struggle against the powers of darkness" (John Paul II, *Mother of the Redeemer*, p.67) guiding the youth in becoming a faithful disciple of Jesus. Father Roger Mercurio, C.P., writes that "The story of Gabriel spread throughout

Italy and beyond at the very time Catholics were drawing strength from Lourdes and La Salette and from the solemn proclamation of the Immaculate Conception." Gabriel would have appreciated the words written about Our Lady by the very pope who beatified him 50 years later, Pope Saint Pius X : "God could have given us the Redeemer of the human race and the Founder of the Faith in another way than through the Virgin, but since Divine Providence has been pleased that we should have the Man-God through Mary, who conceived Him by the Holy Ghost and bore Him in her womb; it only remains for us to receive Christ from the hands of Mary."

As a religious, Confrater Gabriel shared his appreciation for Christ's mother with his fellow religious, with the shepherd people in the villages, and with constant referrals in his letters. Finally, his long-desired wish of taking a private vow in honor of Mary was allowed by his spiritual director. In the next chapter we shall study more in depth how and why Gabriel made a special fifth vow to spread devotion to Mary in his heart and in the hearts of others—and how Gabriel himself was a living Marian flame of love in the Church! Father Norbert remarked about Gabriel's union with Mary: "Its equal is found, perhaps, only in a few of the greatest saints." (Camillus, *Saint Gabriel, Passionist,* pp.160-161) A constant devotional book that Gabriel loved to read was *The Love of Mary* by a Camaldolese hermit, Father Robert. Another favorite book that Gabriel kept on his night table was *The Glories of Mary* by the founder of the Redemptorists and one of the great Doctors of the Church, Saint Alphonsus Maria de Liguori. Saint Alphonsus wrote for his novices: "And how this great Queen must love the religious who have consecrated their freedom, their life, and everything else to the love of Jesus Christ!" (Theodule Rey-Mermet, *Saint Alphonsus Liguori, Tireless Worker for the Most Abandoned*, pp.445-6) Gabriel drank deeply from Alphonsus' Marian-Christocentric spirituality. A Passionist of our own times recently wrote that Mary's motherhood in Gabriel's life and his exceptional union with her at the Cross empowered him to quickly and successfully become "a *sign* of the holiness and dedication that each Christian is called to become." (Mercurio, *Saint Gabriel Possenti, The Passionists*, p. 74) No wonder Gabriel could convincingly remark to a fellow student, "My HEAVEN is the heart of the Sorrowful Mother." (Wilson, *Saint Gabriel, Student, Passionist, Saint*, p.16)

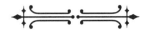

Pause for Reflection

(Excerpt from a letter by Saint Gabriel Possenti to his brother,
December 30, 1861, less than two months before Gabriel's death,
from Burke, *Happy Was My Youth*, pp.184-184)

"Michael, dear, would you like to fall in love? Well then, love if you wish—but whom will you love? Love MARY. Who is more lovely and more lovable, more gracious and powerful? Don't think, just because you cannot actually see her with your eyes, that you'll grow tired of loving Mary, of speaking to her, or spending time with her. On the contrary, the joy and consolation are more pure and lasting, more pleasing to the heart, as much or more so as the soul is above the body, the spirit above the flesh. Note well, furthermore, that no one in this world can make you truly happy. Most people are fickle or false in love. And if you do happen to find one who is true, the mere thought of having to part someday is a bitter torment to the heart. But that never happens to one who chooses Mary. She is loving, faithful, kind; she is never surpassed in love but stays always above all. If you are in danger, she hastens to liberate you; if afflicted, to console you; if sick, to comfort you; if in need, to help you. She never minds what you were in the past. If she but sees a heart that wants to love her, she hastens to it, holds it to her merciful breast, embraces it, protects it, even stoops to serve it, and accompanies it on this brief passage to eternity...Bitter cruel death...in that dread hour, true lovers of Mary are glad of heart. They invite death to draw near and part in peace from their family and from the world. They know that they will soon possess in truth the object of their pure love

AT THE CROSS WITH MARY

and, in her presence, they will be forever happy. Perhaps this letter of mine will make you smile, but I don't mind ... at least I'd like you to know that what I've written comes from the bottom of my heart."

The above writing of Saint Gabriel to his brother, Michael, is truly a "love letter" about the Virgin Mary and what she means in Gabriel's life. For Gabriel, Mary was the great gift of the Crucified Jesus' Last Will and Testament from the Cross. Gabriel cultivated a monastery garden specifically to produce flowers for Mary's altar in both the upstairs choir and the monastery church. If flowers were few, he went off into the countryside, seeking more from the neighbors. In winter he had made room indoors for potted plants and watched over them carefully. A young shepherd boy donated a bouquet of violets for Mary's shrine, and Gabriel was thrilled by the child's generosity. Gabriel grieved over pictures or statues of Mary that were ugly or inexpressive—much like Saint Bernadette. Finding a disheveled, broken statue of Our Lady in an old closet, Gabriel took on the task of repairing it with attention and love, enlisting the help of his peers. He was completely confident that Mary comes to her faithful children at the hour of death to escort them to Heaven, "when we have our soul in our teeth," as he astutely commented. Whenever problems arose he had a saying, "Dearest Mother, take care of it!" Gabriel went through the countryside proclaiming Mary's glories or teaching about her in the little sermons he gave to the students in the public chapel during special feasts. The forty days before the Solemnity of Mary's Assumption was his "Little Lent." He fasted from what was most luscious and abundant at that time in Italy—fruit! All this was for his beloved Lady in spiritual sacrifice and for her poor whom he made sure were fed with his unused portion. All these examples were the sincere demonstrations of a lover in action for his Lady! He also desired to freely share that love with others. Perhaps this seems somewhat peculiar to modern readers. However, Gabriel's writing reveals that he was fully aware that even his contemporaries might smile at these Marian convictions and practices. Nonetheless, Gabriel witnesses with self-confidence what he learned of Mary's love in the recesses of his heart. Such love for Mary was purely God's gift. It was the gift of a relationship with Mary right out of Saint John's Gospel when Jesus gifted the beloved disciple with His Mother's presence, and John immediately embraced her as part of his own life; Gabriel's expression of love was essentially a copy of this Gospel scene.

We can also study Gabriel's above letter as a real appreciation of Mary as free from sin. Interestingly, he was writing from a Passionist Retreat that was once an ancient Franciscan friary originally named for the Virgin of the Annunciation; later, the name was changed to that of the Immaculate

Virgin–believed to be the first church in Italy to bear this name. (Farnum, *Saint Gabriel*, p.142) As a woman free from sin, Mary is free from hate, which is the very absence of love. Mary is filled with love, God's love!

God prepared Mary at the onset of her existence to be open to the fullness of His grace so that she could become the living tabernacle of the Incarnate Word! Gabriel's devotion to her as the Immaculate Conception is clear; He convincingly wrote that Mary's love cannot deceive. In stark contrast, he was painfully aware of the brokenness of sin all around him and the potential for human deception in love. He sensed the lack of constancy in human nature. He wrote, too, from the perspective of his own personal losses because of the deaths of so many loved ones.

In Mary, there is a grounding force of fidelity and permanence. She centered Gabriel in God, away from the human fear of death and loss. Mary was a power for him, not of exaggerated devotion that proved to be fruitless and deadening but a living presence of spiritual joy that shared the unending love of Christ with him as only she can do.

Mary's influence in Gabriel's entire journey and his Marian ardor of living in Christ through her is reflected in the book of Ecclesiasticus and is read in the Sacred Liturgy for his feastday, February 27. In these Scriptural words we envision Mary as the Seat of Wisdom, and Mother of Eternal Wisdom, Jesus Christ.

When I was yet young, before I wandered about, I sought for wisdom openly in my prayer. I prayed for her before the Temple, and unto the very end I will seek after her, and she flourished as a grape soon ripe. My heart delighted in her, my foot walked in the right way, from my youth up I sought after her. I bowed down my ear a little and received her. I found much wisdom in myself, and I profited much therein. To Him that giveth me wisdom will I give glory. For I have determined to follow her: I have had a zeal for good, and shall not be confounded. My soul hath wrestled for her, and in doing it, I have been confirmed. I stretched forth my hands on high, and I bewailed my ignorance of her. I directed my soul to her, and in knowledge I found her. I possessed my heart with her from the beginning: therefore I shall not be forsaken. My entrails were troubled in seeking her: therefore shall I possess a good possession. The Lord hath given me a tongue for my reward: and with it I will praise him.
(Eccles. 51:18-30)

The Word of God
Now there stood by the Cross of Jesus His mother and His mother's sister, Mary of Cleophas, and Mary Magdalen. When Jesus therefore had seen His mother and the disciple standing whom He loved, He said to His mother, "Woman, behold, your son." Then He said to the disciple, "Behold, your mother." And from that hour the disciple took her to his own.

(John 19: 25-27)

Closing Prayers

Saint Gabriel's Prayer to Mary for a Happy Death
O Mother of Sorrows, by the anguish and love with which you did stand by the Cross of Jesus, stand by me in my last agony. To your maternal heart, I commend the last three hours of my life. Offer these hours to the Eternal Father in union with the agony of our dear Lord, in atonement for my sins. Offer to the Eternal Father the Most Precious Blood of Jesus Christ mingled with your tears on Calvary so that I may obtain the grace of receiving Holy Communion with the most perfect love and contrition before my death, so that I may breathe forth my soul in the presence of Jesus. Dearest Mother of Sorrows, when the moment of my death has come, present me to Jesus as your child. Amen.

O God, You marked the soul of Saint Gabriel of Our Lady of Sorrows profoundly with the imprint of the sufferings of Christ Your Son and with the sorrows of the Blessed Virgin, His Mother; grant that we, living as he did with our spirit turned towards the mystery of our salvation, make joyful and quick progress on the way of perfection. We ask this in Jesus' Name and through His Holy Spirit. Amen.

(Adapted From Cingolani, C.P., Life and Prayers, p.38)

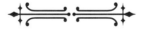

For Further Reflection
The Companionship of Mary

+ Pray over and study Blessed Pope John XXIII's outstanding Gospel meditations on the mysteries of the Rosary. They can be found in his *Journal of a Soul.*

+ Picture in your mind Mary of Nazareth: her household chores, her motherly activities with Jesus, and as wife to Joseph. Dwell on this Gospel portrait for a while. Invite Mary to come to you and to be at your side. Imagine her there with you. Her hands are clasped within yours. Stay with her. Experience her presence in your life.

+ Read Saint Luke's account of Mary's visit to Elizabeth's house. Stay with the story awhile and meditate peacefully on its meaning for you. You can also recall a visit made to you or someone you visited that had a transforming effect on both of you.

+ What does Mary as a model of purity mean for you in today's world? And how is being pure as Jesus prescribed it different than being "puritanical?" Discuss purity of heart and purity of body; are they related and equally important to you? Bring your unified or conflicting ideas to heartfelt prayer with the Heart of Christ.

+ Confrater Gabriel once found an old, neglected, life-size statue of the Sorrowful Mother in a monastery closet. He repaired the broken plaster and repainted it, beautifying the statue. It was placed in a prominent place in the monk's choir chapel and is still there to this day. Creatively renew your thinking of Mary and reestablish your relationship with her.

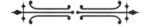

Chapter Thirteen

Belonging to Mary, Being a Flame of Christ for Others

Gabriel's spiritual life was daily maturing in Mary's presence. It gave renewed birth to Christ in his life, a beautiful falling in love with Jesus all over again each day through Mary. Once he was in philosophy studies at Pievetorina, he never wrote of Mary without mentioning Christ. This is the way with Mary, enshrining Christ within our hearts. Mary's perpetual Gospel flame of love for God had penetrated Gabriel's own heart, making him a living Marian fire of love for Christ and His Church. This burning love led Gabriel to give himself at last in a total offering and consecration of self through his solemn vow to Mary, an intensification of his Baptismal vows and his faithful stance at the Cross of Jesus with Mary.

Opening Prayer

O Holy Spirit, give me a great devotion and strong inclination toward Mary, your true Spouse, a secure rest on her maternal breast; and may I have perpetual recourse to her mercy, that by her, You may form in me Jesus Christ, strong and mighty to the fullness of His perfect age. Amen.

(Saint Louis Marie de Montfort, *Treatise on the True Devotion to the Blessed Virgin Mary*, p. 236).

The great day had come at last, Gabriel's Marian offering of self, the fifth vow he longed to make, and had asked permission to make for five years. His spiritual director, Father Norbert, himself a great Mariologist–

having completed his own treatise on the spirituality of Mary, had at last consented, believing without a doubt that Gabriel was ready, mature and destined to be Mary's modern knight in a world that sorely needed the gift which Mary is destined to bring–Christ's overflowing love. It is the love that Christ pined for–begging hearts not to be tepid and non-committed, but aflame with His burning love ignited on the Wood of the Holy Cross. Jesus said, *I am come to cast fire on the earth, and what will I but that it be kindled?* (Luke 12:49)

Now the fire of true romance with Jesus and Mary had begun, a romance hard tested in the fire that beautifies precious ores, the fire of penance and charity, of patience and forgiveness, of reconciliation and daily joy in good times and bad–now the hour had come to lay all these fire-tried gifts at the altar of Mary for her and in her to give to Christ. The hour of his final illness and dying, his being barred to Holy Orders, the crushing disappointments–all were near–yet he would offer them all with a generous heart to God with the added grace of this fifth Marian vow. It was offered and taken in the utmost spirit of a lover.

Like his fourth unique vow to promote devotion to the Passion, (first taken by the mystic Founder, Saint Paul of the Cross at the altar of Mary's famous icon in Saint Mary Major in Rome) Gabriel knew that this fifth vow would complement the fourth and enrich it. It was more than "promoting" or "proclaiming" devotion, (apostolic and missionary cored as that is), but also a total identification with the Mystery–a becoming like the mystery, a configuration into the Sacred Passion, and now, into Mary!

So the side chapel of Our Lady was duly decorated with flowers from Gabriel's own garden, the candles glowed before Mary's image, and Gabriel knelt before Father Norbert in this solemn, private ceremony in the stillness of the night of September, 1861. It was most likely the Feast of Our Lady of Sorrows. Confrater Gabriel of the Sorrowful Virgin, his hands placed in the folded hands of the venerable Father Norbert of Saint Mary of the Garden, solemnly and perpetually vowed to promote devotion to the Blessed Virgin Mary. Father Camillus marvelously comments that "...no chivalrous knight ever rose from his accolading with such pride and delight as did Gabriel that evening after he had pledged himself before heaven to be the champion of her who is the fairest of all the daughters of men." (Saint Gabriel, *Passionist*, p.166).

Truly, Gabriel was on fire with Christian love found in the spiritual garden of Mary's example and active presence in his life, and flowering, to be precise, into a life for, in, and with Jesus Christ. This fifth vow was a total consecration of self forevermore, a rite of spiritual passage and giving that lovers always seem to create–signs of genuine love. We know that this ritualistic "sign" of love was a manifestation of both a personal love and also an outward bound directed one, completely missionary and ever vigilant to overflow in deeds of charity to one and all, particularly the poor, the spiritually impoverished, and the Souls in Purgatory–those awaiting the full light of heaven. This Christo-Marian love was so authentic that God allowed one of Gabriel's classmates, Michael Tadini, to experience it for himself and later testify to it. Gabriel was speaking of Mary with a greater awe, joy and intensity than usual. Michael was trying to follow the train of thought and feeling exuding from Gabriel. Suddenly, an actual flame shot out from the area of Gabriel's heart shooting toward Michael. For the rest of his life, Michael would remember that sensation and warmth of the flame of Marian love from Gabriel's heart. (*Saint Gabriel, A Young Man in Love*, p.104). Gabriel calls each of us to be creatively alive in God, to be living flames of Marian love, witnessing to the world the burning love of Jesus Crucified and Risen.

Consideration

In 1858, Saint Bernadette of Lourdes was called by Our Lady to a life of prayer and penance and toward renewal in the living streams of Gospel and Eucharistic life. Through Bernadette, the world was alerted to this heavenly invitation. Two years before, Gabriel had been called by the Voice of Our Lady of the Icon to the same intensified program. He was living the message as a Passionist during the actual Lourdes apparitions and he died in the year of their ecclesiastical approval. Gabriel died on February 27, the 4th anniversary of one of the eighteen Lourdes apparitions—a day Bernadette had again washed in the spring and kissed the ground in pen-

ance. With Our Blessed Mother, Bernadette and Gabriel both call us to penance, prayer and total self-giving!

Pause for Reflection

"Jesus invites us to pray through her...If we do not let ourselves be won over by the countenance of Mary, we will perhaps agree to the Reign of Jesus, but not to the folly, the folly of the Cross. When we proclaim Mary as Queen, we use the...language of lovers: the Father is seeking worshipers, that is, people who are mad with love...Saint Grignion de Montfort says again that the apostles of the end time will be great saints...' they shall be a burning fire, ministers of the Lord who will kindle the fire of Jesus' Divine Love everywhere...' ".

(LaFrance, *In Prayer with Mary, Mother of Jesus*, pp. 309-310)

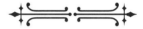

Saint Gabriel stands out as truly one of those great saints and apostles of Mary prophesized by Saint Louis Marie Grignion de Montfort. Gabriel's fifth vow to promote devotion to Mary, an action and gift of self to be identified with her at the Cross, and to be configured into her and her spirituality, is not the exact formula of Saint Louis de Montfort's Consecration but is amazingly akin to its all-giving Marian nature and total surrender. In this surrender of Gabriel, we can see the likeness to the Holy Slavery of Love proposed by the Total Consecration of Saint Louis, a consecration lived also by the servant of God, John Paul II. Saint Louis' *Treatise on True Devotion to Mary* was discovered in 1841 after being buried during the French Revolution to protect it from sacrilege and harm. It is a Marian Consecration that is also a complete giving to Jesus Christ in the renewal of one's Baptismal vows, trustingly giving Mary literally everything we have. Surely Gabriel would have known of this Montfortian Consecration and discussed it at length with his Jesuit professors and peers in the intensely Catholic academic circles of Spoleto. Gabriel was the knight, slave and son of Mary. He desired, like a valiant hero, to engrave Mary's Holy Name on his chest over his own heart, burning it there like her slave and possession! He wanted to write his Marian Credo in his own blood. Father Norbert forbade all these extremely penitential and intensely romantic expressions that had a somewhat Victorian flair or were perhaps even Gothic in nature. He did consent, however, for Gabriel to paint Mary's Holy Name over his heart. Importantly, Father Norbert re-directed Gabriel to an ever increasing purification and refurbishing of his mind and heart to the inner sanctum of the soul—where a real suitable throne could be prepared for Mary. For Gabriel, as in the spirituality of Saint Louis de Montfort, and of course—Saint Paul of the Cross–Mary and the Cross are never separated.

Louis de Montfort wrote of being a "Friend of the Cross," and is most often depicted with the Crucifix in his arms. To be a voluntary slave for Christ and Mary is to give us true freedom from the slavery of the Evil One and to become truly *friends* with God. This loving offering and slavery of freedom is biblically rooted. Saint Paul the Apostle is constantly using the concept and imagery of "slavery" to explain the inter-play between slavery to sin and being freed in Christ, and likewise being a slave of God and experiencing true freedom and friendship in Christ. In slavery to God (Romans 6:16, 22) and His Goodness, we become royal heirs to the inheritance of Christ. We share in Christ's priesthood, royalty, prophecy–becoming children of God and of the Light. Gabriel understood the freedom of this self-giving at the Cross with and in Mary. Reconciliation, peace and freedom come to us in following and also becoming like Christ Who humbled Himself, *Who emptied Himself, taking the form of a servant* (Philippians 2:7). This "emptying" of self like Christ is the core of the Passionist-Precious Blood, Marian and Christian spirituality; herein is true rebirth and saving wholeness. Like the great Marian heroes—Saints Louis de Montfort, Alphonsus Maria de Liguori, Anthony Mary Claret, John Bosco, Bernadette of Lourdes, John Eudes, Dominic Savio, Maximillian Maria Kolbe, and Blessed William Chaminade, (who used his own unique Consecration formula)—Gabriel discovered the self-giving Mary at the emptying of Christ on the Cross and he found Christ in Mary's pierced, maternal and Gospel heart. Another like soul was the heroine of the suffering and dying, Venerable Mary Potter, (who based her spirituality and work on Louis de Montfort's ideology). Each of these saintly members above had in some unique but similar way, made a total, living consecration of their lives to and with Jesus Crucified and through, in and by Mary. (In a riveting discovery for me, the life and spirit of the Marian consecrated life of the Spanish Venerable Maria Teresa Quevedo who died in 1950, is a striking female counterpart to the Marian spirituality and total trust evidenced in Saint Gabriel).

The Word of God

Give ear, my son, and take wise counsel, and cast not away my advice. Put your feet into her fetters and your neck into her chains: bow down your shoulder and bear her, and be not grieved with her bands.

Come to her with all your mind, and keep her ways with all your power. Search for her and she shall be made known to you, and when you have gotten her, let her not go: for in the latter end you shall find rest in her, and she shall be turned to your joy.

Then shall her fetters be a strong defense for you, and a firm foundation, and her chain a robe of glory: for in her is the beauty of life, and her bands are a healthful binding. You shall put her on as a robe of glory, and you shall set her upon yourself as a crown of joy.

(Eccles. 6:24-32)

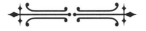

Closing Prayers

An Act of Dedication to the Blessed Virgin Mary
My Queen and Mother, I give myself entirely to you, and in proof of my affection, I give you my eyes, my ears, my tongue, my heart, my whole being without reserve. Since I am your own, keep me and guard me as your property and possession. Amen.

(Watkins, *North American College Manual of Prayers*, Rome p. 79)

An Act of Consecration by Saint Anthony Mary Claret
O Virgin and Mother of God, I surrender myself to you as your child, and in honor and glory of your purity, I offer you my soul and body, my mind and senses, and ask that you obtain for me the grace to avoid all sin. Amen. (Then repeat three times:) Mother Behold your son! (or daughter!) Continue with: I have placed my trust in you, good Mother, and I shall not be confounded. Amen.

(Vinas, Ed., *Autobiography of Saint Anthony Mary Claret*, p. 170)

Short Formula for the Montfortian Offering of Self
Totus Tuus Ego Sum! All that I am is yours, O Jesus, in and through and with Mary, Virgin Most Blessed! I give myself as Mary's true slave in love and freedom, and I promise to carry my cross after You, my Lord Jesus, all the days of my life, to renew and intensify my Baptismal commitment, and to be more faithful to You than I have ever been before. Mary, my Mother and Queen of all Hearts, I give all I am and do and merit, united to the Passion of Jesus to whomever and for whatever maternal cause you

deem best. I trust in you and know you will secure for me the inheritance of the children of God that flows from the Most Precious Blood of the Redeemer, Jesus Christ. Amen.

(Adapted by the Author from the *Treatise and the Spirit of True Devotion* by Saint Louis Marie de Montfort)

For Further Reflection
Belonging to Mary, Being a Flame of Christ for Others.

+ Christ desired a burning love to overtake the world, stemming from His Crucified Love that gives life, joy, peace and forgiveness to our restless souls. How do we keep alive the flame of His Love in our lives, our vocation, our priesthood, married, or single life? Ask Mary who always was ablaze in Jesus' awesome Love, to guide us on His Way.

+ Read the Treatise or a book explaining the Consecration of Saint Louis Marie de Montfort. Is this something special as an avenue of grace for you? Perhaps God is calling you to another type of Marian Consecration or giving of yourself ANEW to JESUS through Mary in your own unique manner. With your spiritual director, or a special friend in the spiritual life, seek how Mary can re-vivify your life in Christ and service to His Kingdom.

+ Spend a prayerful hour, without distractions, before a crucifix. Look at Jesus through the eyes and Heart of Mary. What do you see? What does He say to you? Where does He lead you?

+ Is your life missing meaning and purpose? Saint Maria de Mattias, Foundress of the Precious Blood Missionary Sisters, said, "You are worth the Blood of Jesus!" Place yourself in a time of prayer under the mantle of Our Lady of the Precious Blood; remember your worth, made worthy in Jesus' all giving Sacrifice–you who were entrusted to Mary through the Apostle Saint John, who represented each of us at the Cross.

+ Confidently ask Saint Gabriel to inflame your heart and being with a bit of the fire that emanated from his heart and touched his friend Michael for the rest of his life. Gabriel will bring you to a more vivifying expression of your love for Mary and the living out of your Faith handed down to us by the Apostles.

+ Read the life of Venerable Maria Teresa Quevedo, *Mary Was Her Life*. She is a beautiful soul that was totally consecrated to Jesus and Mary in tremendous joy and charity. She died at age 20. She closely resembles Saint Gabriel's life, vocation, and spirituality.

+ Explore the message of penance and prayer that Our Lady of Lourdes calls us to live and be in the Church and in the world.

Chapter Fourteen

Believing When Dreams are Broken

Confrater Gabriel was called upon by disappointments and illness to
enter his own personal "Garden of Gethsemane"; he increased his hope
when the priestly dream was thwarted, struggled to became one with the
Father's will when he realized he was dying, and reshaped his original
vision—focusing on the Lord's love and promises—even in the empty
hole of pain and darkness.

Opening Prayer
*"My Saviour! I cheerfully accept all the painful dispositions, in which
it is Thy pleasure to place me. My wish is in all things to conform myself
to Thy holy will. Whenever I kiss Thy Cross, it is to show that I submit
perfectly to mine."*
(St. Margaret Mary Alacoque, *Prayer in Resignation to Suffering*)

It was December, 1861. The giant peaks of Gran Sasso were covered
in snow. Gabriel's cough had acutely worsened. At times, the pain ripped
through his chest. It was becoming more and more difficult to ascend the
steps leading to his room. Early to mid-November, Gabriel had his first attack of hemoptysis, (the coughing up of blood) and he was diagnosed with
advanced pulmonary tuberculosis, an incurable disease in his day.

Akin to Saint Therese, who shared the same illness and who also died
at the age of twenty-four, Gabriel and Therese's sentiments appear to be the
same: they readjusted their vocational plans and put all their spiritual hope

upon seeing the object of their love in heaven. Their belief in the Risen Lord was undaunted! They united their suffering to the priestly offering of Christ's one offering of self on the Cross and prayed for the world at large. They were not going to waste this precious gift of suffering love. They were not going to become bitter and ruined because their young aspirations appeared destroyed! This was the time of testing, of choices, of proving their vowed identity with the Man of Sorrows, Jesus, the Lord. Neither saint achieved holiness within a vacuum; they reached out for support and love. Therese poured out her heart to her intimately bonded blood sisters! Gabriel entrusted these dark hours to Father Norbert.

Indeed, Gabriel was now called to be a Passionist in its fullest meaning! In fact, it was at this juncture when he saw his youthful life ebbing away toward death and the priesthood denied to him that he had to enter his personal Garden of Gethsemane...*Abba, Father ... not what I will, but what You will.* (Mark 14: 36) Gabriel could have run back home, given up on God, and deserted his vocation. In sad contrast, one of his classmates did eventually leave the Passionists, the priesthood and the Faith itself. (Burke, *Happy Was My Youth*, p.122). Instead, Gabriel walked through a frightening experience on his own road to Calvary. The pain was at times unbearable–with bouts of suffocation and vomiting. His fellow religious had to begin assisting him with his walking, as he leaned on their arms. Towards the end, they took turns keeping watch at his bedside; Gabriel insisted that these thoughtful night-watchers get more sleep during the day, or else, as he suggested, take shorter intervals and switch off more frequently with other monks. This is also a spirit very much akin to Saint Bernadette in her illness, and her concern for her "watchers."

The country people expressed their concern, too. Egidio Ottaviani of a nearby town, Pacciano, had fresh milk delivered everyday for the dying student. Gabriel was really grateful, and he earnestly prayed to Mary, "My Mother, will you remember to reward him? Give him every grace he needs for soul and body." (Burke, p. 238) Gabriel didn't want to wear others down with complaints of constant discomfort and pain. He attempted to keep a sense of humor throughout the harrowing illness. When asked how he was feeling by others, he usually joked, "Much the same as usual–like the blind beggar!" (Ibid, p. 240) When Norbert called in all the available specialists to save the youth, the wasting student did all he could to remain gracious and compliant with their limited treatments. He was at first adverse to a last resort of one of the doctors who wanted to apply two plasters to the chest. After recollecting his thoughts in prayer, Gabriel said, "...I take back what I said. If they want to put on the plasters, let them go ahead. I'm ready for them!" (Ibid, p. 237)

Upon reading Gabriel's life, we could easily concentrate on Gabriel's charming personality, his patience, and his desire for Heaven, about which he often and unabashedly talked. We can't forget that his was a faith without sight, and a belief within "the dark night of the soul"–as Saint John of the Cross described it. No doubt, Gabriel spoke of hope and peaceful moments of grace, but he also knew anguish, grief, horrifying temptations to the Faith, and the humiliation of increased debilitation when prevented from being able to do things for himself. He told Father Norbert exactly what his daily prayer and offering would now literally become: "O My Jesus, I offer you love for love, suffering for suffering, blood for blood..." (Poage, *Son of the Passion*, p. 99)

Now, more than ever, his devotion to Our Lady of Sorrows proved to be real. Gabriel wrote: "That loving Virgin of Sorrows, who cannot behold our misery without compassion, holds us in peace beneath her mantle." (Burke, p. 222) He gave Mary his disappointments, sharing his own with the ones she experienced on earth. He related that six events in his own life corresponded to the seven sorrows which Mary is traditionally believed to have suffered. Gabriel confided to Norbert alone the seventh one; it was going to be his painful death. We can speculate that four sorrows must have been the death of his own mother, and of his siblings–Paul, Lawrence, and Maria Luisa. The fifth and sixth sorrows were probably the loss of never seeing his father again and the inevitable loss of the priesthood. Gabriel confided to Francis, his friend in medical school, "I shall no longer be alive when you have made a name for yourself as a doctor." (Burke, p. 226) With Jesus, Gabriel could actually declare: *My soul is sorrowful even to death.*

(Mark 14: 34)

Consideration
Ill that He blesses is our good,
And unblest good is ill;
And all is right that seems most wrong,
If it be His sweet Will.

(Father William Faber)

Pause for Reflection
For God, Who commanded the light to shine out of darkness, has shined in our hearts to give the light of the knowledge of the glory of God, in the face of Christ Jesus. But we have this treasure in earthen vessels, that the excellency may be of the power of God, and not of us. In all things we suffer tribulation, but are not distressed; we are straightened, but not destitute; we

suffer persecution, but are not forsaken; we are cast down, but we perish not: always bearing about in our body the mortification of Jesus, that the life also of Jesus may be made manifest in our bodies. For we who live are always delivered unto death for Jesus' sake that the life also of Jesus may be made manifest in our mortal flesh...For which cause we faint not: but though our outward man is corrupted, yet the inward man is renewed day by day. For that which is at present momentary and light of our tribulation, works for us above measure exceedingly an eternal weight of glory....While we look not at the things which are seen, but at the things which are not seen. For the things which are seen are temporal, but the things which are not seen are eternal.

(II Corinthians 4:6-11; 16-18)

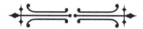

Father Norbert, who knew Gabriel's heart and mind so well, reflected on his spiritual son's enthusiasm for missionary and priestly life as a Passionist. He optimistically wrote to Gabriel's father in May, 1861: "I can almost promise you he will sing his first Mass on Christmas Day. Let us hope in God and offer fervent prayers." (Ibid, p. 202) That May, Gabriel and his classmates received tonsure and minor orders in the Cathedral at Peme. It was a very happy day. However, the war for Italy's unity intensified, and all immediate plans for major orders were dropped by the bishop; traveling had become perilous. This was not the only thing that prevented Gabriel's ordination. For him, it was not a delay, as for the other students. Gabriel's tuberculosis was barring him permanently from ordained priesthood; he was dying and consequently that particular dream would never materialize. Gabriel wrote home in December, leaving out the disturbing news of his illness: "At this time, perhaps, I would have been a priest...Since God wills it thus, I will it too." (Ibid, p. 201) Short as this phrase is, there is in it the same spirit of the making of ALL the saints: their resignation to God's designs and their primary attachment to God alone—never accomplished effortlessly or without a great human price of hurt and mourning.

Saint Jane Frances de Chantal wrote, that at the time she was about to learn that her beloved friend Saint Francis de Sales had died, and before reading the letter, which contained the news, "I withdrew myself into God and into His holy will." (Henry Couannier, *Saint Francis de Sales and His Friends*, p. 392) However, later that night, Saint Jane wept in her room. We can only ponder how much Saint Gabriel must have wept in the privacy of his own monastic cell.

Confrater Gabriel's missionary goal to preach and reach out to a far wider audience would not be fulfilled in "his way' but would be amazingly achieved in God's own magnificent and surprising manner. In the encroaching cold of January, 1862, Father Norbert noticed Gabriel taking a prayerful, wintry walk in the monastery garden. After Gabriel had passed by his particular flowerbed that he had so often tended in good weather, Father Norbert noticed a red rose blooming—one that was not there the day before! Father Norbert believed that this was a holy sign of the great prodigies to come through Gabriel's heavenly intercession. (Lucas, p. 89) After Gabriel's dark passage into death, his ministry would explode beyond the boundaries of Gran Sasso and encircle the globe through his influence and intercession to aid countless people of God. Indeed, God's servant Gabriel was *strengthened by His Spirit with might unto the inward man* and glorified by Him *Who is able to do all things more abundantly than we desire or understand.* (Ephesians 3:16,20)

The Word of God

And going out He went according to His custom to the Mount of Olives, and His disciples followed Him. And when He was come to the place, He said to them, "Pray, lest you enter into temptation." And He was withdrawn away from them a stone's cast, and kneeling down He prayed saying, "Fa-

ther, if You will, remove this chalice from Me; but yet not My will but Yours be done." And there appeared to Him an angel from Heaven, strengthening Him. And being in an agony He prayed the longer. And His sweat became as drops of blood, trickling down upon the ground.

(Luke 22: 39-44)

Closing Prayer

The mercies of the Lord that we are not consumed, because His commiserations have not failed. They are new every morning, great is Thy faithfulness. The Lord is my portion, and my soul; therefore will I wait for Him. The Lord is good to them that hope in Him, to the soul that seeks Him. It is good to wait with silence for the salvation of God. It is good for a man when he has borne the yoke from his youth. He shall sit solitary and hold his peace, because he has taken it up upon himself. He shall put his mouth in the dust, if so be there may be hope. He shall give his cheek to them that strike him; he shall be filled with reproaches. For the Lord will not cast off forever. For if He cast off, He will also have mercy, according to the multitude of His mercies. For He has not willingly afflicted or cast off the children of men.

(Lamentations 3:22-33)

For Further Reflection
In The Forge of God's Love

+ Looking back on a disappointment in your life, can you now see any good that developed out of it? What did you learn or how did you grow? For some, the broken dream might have set off a chain of events that lead to a particularly successful outcome. Whatever your personal situation, reflect on God's loving designs in your life giving Him thanks and praise.

+ Reverently read one of the Evangelist's Passion accounts. Before the open pages of the Gospel, confidently lift up your sufferings, illnesses, and discouragements to the Heavenly Father and pray for His glory united to Jesus' one priestly offering on the Cross and renewed in every Mass. Pray deeply with and for the whole Church. Pray for God's will to be fulfilled in you!

+ Entreat Saint Gabriel to bless and assist at the bedsides of the terminally ill today—especially those who have been abandoned by their loved ones and friends in their most fearful and desperate hours. May Saint Gabriel's intercession help to move the hearts of others to come to the dying with love and healing presence.

+ Visit a friend or a relative who is ill, or housebound; bring flowers from your garden, a homemade dessert, and especially yourself. Share some moments of prayer with them. Be a sign of God's mercy and care to the sick.

+ Reach out to a disheartened peer who feels that life's opportunities are unreachable or closed off to him/her, or who lacks courage to rethink a new plan and envision another dream. Help them to be aware of the wellspring of resources within their very selves, ready to be tapped. Encourage them to use their creative power to move forward.

+ Pray about raising money for a good cause—perhaps participating in a bake-sale or even a biking marathon! The Lord will open doors of creative service if you seek it!

+ Bring your own losses, whatever they may be, before God. Ask the Lord for healing and new peace. Remember that instead of anger and bitterness, "you can grow in and through the amazing gifts of loss: deeper insight into yourself, your values, and dreams for the future, a heart broken—but also widened to contain more compassion and love…" (Schweska, *The Journey, A Newsletter to Help in Bereavement*, p. 2)

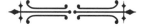

Chapter Fifteen

Dying, Passage to heaven

Confrater Gabriel's passion and death was the completion of his journey leading to paradise. The ultimate, triumphant gift of himself on this planet was his dying hour, his last breath, given up in hope and trust to God, his Father, and the lover of his whole being. On the gibbet of Gabriel's cross, he would find the fullness of the Risen Lord!

Opening Prayer
"Virgin most resigned, although thou didst feel thine own soul transfixed with sorrow, foreseeing all the bitter Passion of thy Son, yet knowing the grief of Joseph thy spouse for all thy sufferings, thou didst console him with holy words; pierce through and through our souls with true sorrow for our sins, that we may one day come to rejoice with thee in everlasting bliss, partakers of thy glory."
(Raccolta, excerpt from *Novena for the Purification*)

It was the eve of February 27, 1862. Gabriel was in enormous respiratory distress. The end was near. Father Norbert kept vigil at his friend's bedside. The young man before him had terribly wasted; his body was emaciated, and his face was gaunt and pale. Gabriel drifted in and out of sleep. Sometimes, he awoke and glanced at the Passionist habit placed over a chair by the bed, the uniform he had worn in honor of Christ Crucified. He had requested that the garb be kept close by, saying it comforted him. Gabriel was sad that the infirmarian would not allow the heavy habit to be actually worn, but he surrendered to this for love of Jesus and Mary. His resistance was low, his body exhausted. However, his will and spirit were still strong, and he was determined to run the race to the finish. (II Tim. 4:7)

As Gabriel was approaching the final stretch of his spiritual journey, it seemed that all the powers of darkness wanted to lash out at him in anger and hatred, attempting to draw the youth back from the glory that would soon be his, away from the eternal Light. Norbert and Gabriel were experienced with the assaults of the Evil One, acutely aware of his activity in the world. They took to heart the admonition: *Be sober and watch because your adversary the devil, as a roaring lion, goes about seeking whom he may devour. Resist him, strong in faith...*(I Peter 5: 8-9)

Twice, Gabriel was shaken by lewd phantasms about his bed while he was making preparatory prayers for a holy death. Both times, Gabriel was visibly disturbed, ordering the images to leave the roam. Norbert, informed of the problem, blessed the room with holy water and prayed over Gabriel for deliverance from evil. After a brief interlude of peace, another fierce attack came; Gabriel was tempted with presumption–an exaggerated conceit that he had won holiness on his own efforts! Resisting the temptation, Gabriel cried aloud to Christ over and over, "Your wounds are my merit!!" (Farnum, *Saint Gabriel*, p.184) Again, the faithful priest and friend at his bedside blessed the room and the dying student, and once more, together, they prayed for peace. The trials ended. Again, Gabriel clung to the picture of the Crucified Jesus.

A beautiful serenity now filled Gabriel's person and in spite of the raging fever and racking cough, joy and confidence replaced fear and perplexity. As his breathing became more labored, Gabriel managed to pray several times to Mary, "My Mother, make haste!" (Farnum, Ibid, p.185) He was calling on the Woman he believed would accompany his soul to his Redeemer. Had he not said almost everyday of his life "Pray for us sinners, now, and at the hour of our death?" Again, he whispered, "My Mother, make haste!" He was definitely letting go. It was the time to leave the world as he had known it. He was going to trust the heavenly Father and Jesus' assurances that he would not be abandoned at this crossover, that God was waiting–around the corner of this earth's limited knowledge and experiences–to embrace him into another, larger sphere of the eternal Presence and the activity of God's love.

It was nearing dawn, Thursday, and it was the observance of the feast of Saint Margaret of Cortona, a Franciscan Third Order penitent, whom Gabriel had always admired and prayed to as a special heavenly friend. (Cavatassi & Giorgini, C.P., Eds., *Fonti Storico-Biografiche*, p.172) He was thinking of her now. He thought of Margaret's conversion to a life of prayer and her graced ability to influence others to turn back to God. He prayed to Margaret to help him be faithful at his own last hour.

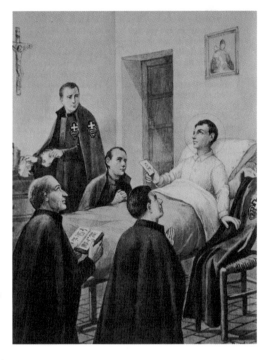

Then, Gabriel turned his attention over to the sketch from his breviary, a drawing of a youthful Christ on the cross with his Sorrowful Mother nearby. He affectionately kissed the picture. Unabashedly, he shed tears of happiness for a life fulfilled in Christ and tears of peaceful joy for the passage he was about to make. Gabriel began to pray very deliberately, "Jesus, Mary and Joseph, I give you my heart and my soul. Jesus, Mary and Joseph, assist me in my last agony. Jesus, Mary and Joseph, may I breathe..." He did not finish the last words "forth my soul in peace with you." "He prolonged the word b-r-e-a-t-h-e ... noticeably ... They were his last words." (Burke, *Happy Was My Youth*, p.252)

Father Norbert quickly directed the bell to be rung to summon the entire community to the dying man's bed to prayerfully accompany their brother in the momentous transition of his spirit. The monks brought lighted candles, symbolizing the light of Jesus. Gabriel's face was suddenly transformed, and glowed in genuine ecstasy, witnessed by all present. (Ibid, p.253) Father Norbert stated that he had never seen such a light on any face either before or after this beautiful "transitus"...a "passing" from this life to the other. Gabriel then managed to lift up his frail body, and his face glanced toward the left, by the window, "although his hands still clasped the little picture as before. Then he gently sank back and expired." (Ibid, p.252) The hour was half-past six. Father Norbert would always be convinced that Mary had come for her son in that very room (Cavatassi & Giorgini, Eds., Ibid, p.172) and escorted him "to that other life for which all his days in the monastery had been an uninterrupted preparation." (Farnum, *Saint Gabriel*, p.186)

Consideration

"Jesus, destroy this chain of a body, for I shall never be content until my soul can fly to You. When shall I be completely blessed in You?"

(Saint Gemma Galgani)

Pause for Reflection

For none of us lives to himself, and no man dies to himself. For whether we live, we live unto the Lord; or whether we die, we die unto the Lord. Therefore whether we live or whether we die, we are the Lord's. For to this end Christ died and rose again, that He might be Lord both of the dead and the living.

(Romans 14: 7-9)

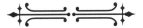

The death of Gabriel may appear at first to be high drama, too pious, saccharine, and too perfect as a final script. Perhaps, we are unmoved by "holy" death scenes rather than inspired because we have been conditioned to whisk away the dying from our sight. Unlike the rest of the world's history before this century, we are no longer regularly called upon to wait on the dying at close quarters in our homes. Our children are not well informed (other than the violent killings they witness in the media) about death's religious meaning and human import. The current and popular use of a fake grass mat, covering a grave at the time of burial, is a good example of the extremes our culture takes to hide the stark reality of death's earthly finality, softening for ourselves the sobering truth of every person's destiny.

Quite differently, Saint Gabriel's dying experience was very natural and human. He was able to talk about impending death to his confreres and friends and prepare for death daily by meditating on and living in Jesus crucified. He had hope for a transformed life to come. He had loving fraternity surrounding his final hours, assisting him in ushering his spirit into another dimension of reality. Gabriel's face, witnessed to be in an aura of light, as well as his body lifting itself up as if to welcome a heavenly presence, are not so unusual if placed within the light of solid faith and tradition.

Saint Gabriel's death offers a model for living well and for dying well as equally important values, especially for the Christian whose very faith hinges on the dogma of the Risen Jesus. *If Christ be not risen again, your faith is in vain, for you are yet in your sins. Then they also who have fallen asleep in Christ are perished. If in this life only we have hope in Christ, we are of all men most miserable.* (I Corinthians 15: 17-19) Gabriel surrendered his every gift into the one crowning gift of himself–allowing God to enfold him in the most mysterious of human experiences–death. Gabriel reached out to death with a valorous and penetrating hope in the fullness of resurrection. Gabriel, crucified in the spirit with Christ, (Galatians 2:19) will surely share in His resurrection! Any human being, like Gabriel, who has been true to his or her inner self and God-given call on this planet– living fully the gift of life–and who has been consciously maturing within the purifying love of the Holy Spirit, will be able to meet death with a particular sense of understanding and peace. The possibility of bitterness, despair, and regret will be severely lessened, if not all together banished.

Those who were at Gabriel's side, not only nurtured their brother, but they learned by witnessing for themselves that the exceptional moment of death is not a perishing thing but a passing over into newness and freedom. They perceived the sacred moment, and many of them would allow the experience to broaden their perspective and insight into death. As we faithfully stand with the dying at their crosses and give them all our love, we also become more believable as Christ's people. We also learn by the loss of loved ones to appreciate life more than ever before. Our hearts are broken but, with faith, stretched wider to open up and embrace others more

AT THE CROSS WITH MARY

sincerely. Our visions widen beyond the boundaries of what we see to the unseen forces all about us. We become crucified with Jesus' life-giving cross and live by the hope His resurrection gives to us.

The Word of God

And it was almost the sixth hour and there was darkness over all the earth until the ninth hour. And the sun was darkened and the veil of the Temple was rent. And Jesus, crying with a loud voice, said, "Father, into Thy hands I commend My spirit." And saying this He gave up the ghost.... And all the multitude that were come together to that sight, and saw the things that were done, returned striking their breast.

(Luke 23: 44-46, 48)

Closing Prayer

We acknowledge Christ the Lord through Whom we hope that our lowly bodies will be made like His in glory, and we say:

Christ, Son of the living God, Who raised up Lazarus, Your friend, from the dead, raise up to life and glory the dead whom You have redeemed by Your Precious Blood.

Christ, Consoler of those who mourn, You dried the tears of the family of Lazarus, of the widow's son, and the daughter of Jairus, comfort those who mourn for the dead.

Christ, Saviour, destroy the reign of sin in our earthly bodies, so that just as through sin we deserved punishment, so through You we may gain eternal life.

Christ, Redeemer, look on those who have no hope because they do not know You may they receive faith in the resurrection and in the life of the world to come.

You revealed yourself to the blind man who begged for the light of his eyes show Your face to the dead who are still deprived of Your light.

When at last our earthy home is dissolved, give us a home, not of earthly making, but built of eternity in Heaven.

Our Father, Who art in Heaven...

(Intercessions, Office for the Dead, Evening Prayer,
Liturgy of the Hours, Vol. III, p. 1910)

I am the root and offspring of David, the bright morning star... The Spirit and the bride say: Come. And he that hears, let him say: Come. And he that thirsts, let him come: and he that will, let him take the water of life freely.

(Apoc. 22: 16-17)

For Further Reflection
New Life in the Risen Jesus

+ Gabriel's director, Father Norbert, was a friend of the optimist and teacher of youth, Saint John Bosco (Burke, *Happy Was My Youth*, p. 84). Don Bosco recommended to all a consideration of the last hours on earth and regular prayers for a happy death in the Lord. Think about your own last hours. Where do you want to be, emotionally and spiritually at that appointed time before death? Are you prepared if at this moment God were to summon you?

+ Ask the Holy Spirit for the gift of becoming a healing presence for a dying person in your family or community. Pray especially for the courage and peacefulness of *standing by the Cross of Jesus* (John 19:25) in someone's dying hour.

+ Saint Gabriel was surnamed by his companions as the "Apostle of Purgatory" (Hage, *Saint Gabriel of Our Lady of Sorrows,* p. 221) because he always recommended prayers to and for the Holy Souls. With Saint Gabriel, pray for and with these souls in their maturation in God's love.

+ Find a secluded spot for yourself; recall a person you loved who has died. Remember their voice, their touch, and the fine memories you shared. See them at your side. Experience their closeness to you within the Communion of Saints with Jesus as the unbreakable link between the two of you. Speak to your beloved the words of Scripture: *What will separate us from the love of Christ?*

+ Many people have a hard time understanding the intercessory role of the saints in Heaven, those faithful friends of the Lord! However, we all pray for one another! We all share in the work of redemption won for us by our Saviour. Jesus calls us to be sharers of His redeeming grace. It is family. We are part and parcel of His gift-giving and gift-bearing. Let us pray for the world in need of our prayers and ask the saints who have gone before us to help us on the way of salvation!

AT THE CROSS WITH MARY

Chapter Sixteen

Love Beyond the Grave

Saint Gabriel's story was revealed to the people of God, and his name was glorified; he was given an extraordinary ministry of love, one of physical and spiritual healing to perform for those in need. His humble discipleship in the footsteps of Jesus had reaped a success beyond expectation; Gabriel's own written words as a student had become prophetic: "To acknowledge oneself to be a fool is to become wise with the wisdom of God and to be raised to a throne of spiritual power."

(Burke, *Happy Was My Youth*, p. 166)

Opening Prayer

Lord Jesus, crucified and risen, You taught Saint Gabriel to cling to You alone as Lord and Saviour and to find in Your Mother a refuge and companion along the Gospel way. You revealed his sanctity to a world growing cold in love for You and showed him to us as an example of humbly listening to Your call and courageously following the light of Your Holy Spirit. You exalted Gabriel by virtues, even to the working of miracles! Through his prayers and example, may we, too, who honor him, share in the marvelous joys of friendship with You and the Blessed Virgin, and come to the heavenly Father in eternal glory, where You live forever and ever. Amen.

In 1866, Victor Emmanuel suppressed religious congregations. Thus the Passionist Retreat of the Immaculate Conception, where Saint Gabriel had died four years earlier, was abandoned. He lay in the damp crypt beneath the church on the bare ground. Like Saint Therese, his body was reduced to a skeleton. Its form lay with his arms, once folded over his breast, now open as upon a cross—his left hand enmeshed with the skeletal hands of another student, Confrater Peter of Holy Mary, who had died a holy death four years before Gabriel. Gabriel had once expressed a holy envy at Peter's beautiful sanctity and resignation at death. They had been buried next to each other and no coffins were used. The corpses were simply laid on the ground with a brick under each head.

Mysteriously now they shared a symbolic solidarity in the tomb. Gabriel's leather cincture was intact, as was his Sign; there were also parts of his rosary, his profession crucifix, and a Miraculous Medal he had worn. All these items were later found upon opening the crypt. The people of the mountain region of the Gran Sasso did not forget the memory of their much-loved seminarian, Confrater Gabriel. His grave had become a place of prayer and devotion. His holiness was felt among them as well as his ongoing prayers for their well being.

While Father Norbert worked diligently among his Passionist brethren to spread his convictions that Gabriel was indeed a saint, the country folk were already invoking his intercessory power before God. On October 17, 1892, when the process for canonization was officially opened, a secret commission arrived at Isola del Gran Sasso to exhume the body of Gabriel Possenti and bring it to a more accessible location. To their astonishment, as if the Spirit had summoned them, about four thousand people were drawn to the monastery to protect their hidden treasure. They made it clear that the *Santino* (little saint) was remaining with them! A delegation was set up from each township in order to oversee the investigation of the holy remains.

On October 18, the treasured bones of Confrater Gabriel were placed in a double casket and interred in a new space near the side altar where the Passionist founder was buried. On October 23, the first documented and officially accepted miracle was rendered through Saint Gabriel's prayers and the use of his relics. See more details in the Introduction. After this, the physical miracles and spiritual conversions were legion! Many took the dust from the original crypt where Gabriel's body had rested for so many years; through this, the Lord of all Miracles wrought many wonders in honor of His faithful "Son of the Passion" and true "Apostle of Mary." By 1897, ninety cases of complete and instantaneous cures were recorded: cripples left their chairs to walk, the blind could see again, and the deaf heard. Many interior healings of the heart and mind took place. In that year, a second exhumation of the body was undertaken. A mysterious fungus type

S. GABRIELE DELL'ADDOLORATA
Passionista

plant but beautifully shaped as a lily surrounded all the bones in the casket. It was believed by many to represent Gabriel's great purity and struggle to maintain it as well as his Marian devotion. This plant was divided and distributed to the faithful. Fathers Paul Anthony and Romuald both discovered two pellets in the skull that were perfectly contoured and preserved. Father Paul Anthony remarked that he was instantly struck by the thought that *"Mary wished to conserve the instrument of holy thought of him who always had her in his mind!"*

The small shrine in the mountains mushroomed into a powerhouse of prayer; it is often called "Gabriel's Mission." People traveled for miles to seek the saintly youth's assistance with their problems and infirmities; they found much more. Under Gabriel's guidance, they found Christ again in their lives! Invoking Gabriel's patronage seemed to entail a subsequent return to the sacraments and a life of conversion to the Lord. Most of the physical healings were combined with a profound inner transformation, a need for the Sacrament of Penance, and the reception of the Eucharist. This was gospel territory! It manifested the Spirit and work of Jesus within His own disciple, Gabriel, and among God's people. Gabriel had opened up a daily mission for the proclamation of Jesus Crucified, Mary most Holy, and the healing of the body and the soul!

Gabriel's force of love for Christ and Mary in his hidden life as a monk was most fully revealed in an explosion of posthumous ministry. Never ordained, he was nonetheless exercising a type of mystical and priestly ministry and became one of the most effective Passionist mission preachers ever known, and this–beyond the limitations of the grave!

Miracles less known in most biographies are presented here to show the extent of the wondrous renewal of Gospel life through Gabriel's intercession. A man, named Cajetan Mariani of Amatrice, was severely paralyzed for twelve years due to a stroke. He was seventy-one years old and had no hope for a cure. Furthermore, the embittered Cajetan had been estranged from God, the Church, and its sacraments for a very long time. However, by some "unaccountable impulse," he went to the shrine at Isola. He saw the vast crowds praying at the tomb of Gabriel a long line of penitents going to confession nearby. He was deeply inspired and moved to have his confession heard. Many of the people there knew of this angry man and were surprised that he had come to a church, never mind that he was approaching the sacrament! When he finally emerged from the confessional, hunched over on his cane, as usual, walking with difficulty, his eyes were filled with tears and a new serenity was written all over his face. He had returned to Christ! It was truly a very special miracle. But there is more to tell. A few days later, Cajetan returned to the shrine; he was fully cured of all his physical ailments! He sought out the Passionist priest and said, "O Father, this dear servant of God obtained three great graces for me: he touched my heart and brought me back to God. I have prayed and felt myself cured all at once of my paralysis, so that I am well and can walk about with ease, you see; besides, I was afflicted for many years with rupture; this, too, has disappeared this very hour. What shall I do to show my gratitude to God for so many blessings?" (Lummer, C.P. *Saint Gabriel of Our Lady of Sorrows*, p. 27)

Another man, Anthony Mancini, grossly crippled and deformed for many years by arthritis decided to journey to Gabriel's monastery to ask for healing. It was 1893. He had to be carried strapped into a chair in the open wagon for fear that any jolt of the wagon might make him fall out of his seat. The various villages which witnessed this procession were moved to pity for him. Upon arriving at the tomb at evening time, he was given lodgings. In the morning he was carried to the sepulcher. The parish priest heard Anthony's confession and gave him Communion. Then Anthony fervently prayed to Gabriel. All at once he rose from his chair—healed!! "Gabriel, the Servant of God, granted me this favor!" He got into the wagon unaided for the ride home. Each village through which he had passed before was enthralled to see him return as a healthy man; the people from each town gathered to behold this wonder and hear the miraculous story. (Hage, pp. 261-3)

A monastery of Capuchin nuns was making a novena to the Servant of God, Gabriel of the Sorrowful Virgin, for the healing of their beloved Sister Concetta of Saint Michael; she had suffered many years with an ulcer that had brought her to the point of death. During the novena, Sister's condition worsened. At the commencement of the second novena,

Saint Gemma Galgani

the sick nun's condition seemed to climax. Relentlessly, the community began the third novena! A little after midnight of the first day of this last novena, Sister Concetta relates that her entire cell was filled with brilliant light. Within a bright globe stood the most beautiful young man attired in a black robe with a dazzling white surplice. His face was brighter and more radiant than his encircling glory. It was Gabriel. He drew near to her bed. "Are you not going to ask me for something?" he said. Sister replied, "Yes, give me what Mother Abbess wants me to have: cure me." Then Gabriel touched her. Sister Concetta felt that she was free from all pain in that moment. "I thought I was in Heaven both in soul and in body, so great was the consolation I felt." She arose from her bed, totally healed. Meanwhile, Gabriel was slowly withdrawing from the room—leaving Sister Concetta in absolute peace and joy. (Hage, pp 267-69)

Saint Gemma, a lay stigmatist and Passionate associate, had many wonderful visitations from our Gabriel! He would often sit on the edge of her bed and recite the Breviary with her, counsel her, and sometimes scold her for some slight imperfection—but with brotherly charity! Once, he removed his Passionist Sign from his habit, placed it over her heart, and said, "My sister!" Gemma relates that Gabriel's guardian angel, who watched over him during his earthly journey, would visit her and tell her beautiful things or announce Gabriel's coming. Gemma also related that Gabriel's angel was far more beautiful than her own angel or that of her confessor, Venerable Father Germanus. (Father Germanus was the promoter of the Cause for Gabriel's canonization.) Another time, Gemma saw Gabriel with a smiling face in a vision; he was adoring the Blessed Sacrament while being bathed in heavenly light.

Importantly, many other wondrous miracles have been wrought to the benefit of children and young people. As in his earthly life, but now as a great intercessory power in Heaven, Gabriel was and is manifesting the

Gospel power of healing and conversion the Lord Himself promised us that we will be able to exercise if we are in union with Him.

Consideration

"...I understand also that in heaven I will fulfill in my turn a priesthood over your soul. It is Love which associates me with His work in you..."
(Blessed Elizabeth of the Trinity, excerpt of her letter to Mother Germaine, from *Elizabeth of the Trinity, I Have Found God*. The Complete Works, Vol. I, p.30)

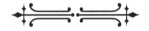

Pause for Reflection

But the souls of the just are in the hands of God, and the torment of death shall not touch them. In the sight of the unwise they seemed to die, and their departure was taken for misery, and their going away from us, for utter destruction, but they are in peace. And though in the sight of men they suffered torments, their hope is full of immortality. Afflicted in few things, in many they shall be well rewarded, because God has tried them, and found them worthy of Himself. As gold in the furnace, He has proved them, and as a victim of holocaust, He has received them, and in time there shall be respect had to them. The just shall shine and shall run to and fro like sparks among the reeds. They shall judge nations and rule over people, and their Lord shall reign forever. They that trust in Him shall understand the truth, and they that are faithful in love shall rest in Him, for grace and peace is to His elect.

(Wisdom 3: 1-9)

When Gabriel Possenti was nearing death, Father Norbert–totally convinced of the glory and activity of love in the "life to come"–reminded his spiritual son: "When you are in Heaven, will you remember to say a little prayer for us? We have all been together in this world and we want to be all together in Heaven. The one who gets there first will have to take care of those who are coming later." Gabriel smiled to his friend. He promised that he would comply with Norbert's request by God's grace and Mary's help. (Burke, *Happy Was My Youth*, pp. 241-242)

Saint Therese, like her Carmelite sister, Elizabeth of the Trinity, had a penetrating insight into what her loving actions would be like after death. God would not abandon her manifold desires to serve and preach His sacred Name. She would save souls and lead the world further into and closer to the Light of Christ. Therese explained, "I can't think very much about the happiness of Heaven; only one expectation makes my heart beat, and it is the love I shall receive, and I shall be able to give. And then I think of all the good I would like to do after my death: have little children baptized, help priests, help missionaries, and help the whole Church... But first console my little sisters." (Clarke, Trans., *Saint Therese of Lisieux, Her Last Conversations*, p.94) She also said to Mother Agnes that she wouldn't always send what the others expected– "ripe plums"–but that she might bring the contrary, such as "great trials," if God thought it was best for them, "but I'll send you lights which will make you appreciate and love them." (Ibid.)

In retrospect, both Gabriel and Therese have shown the Church that the saints are alive in God's love, ministering that love as exceptional missionaries of Christ. The saints are concerned persons who are not remote and uninvolved. Their splendid existence in Paradise does not lessen their bonds to earth; rather, they appear closer and more able than ever before to exercise the powers Christ promised his disciples.

The Word of God

Amen, amen I say to you, he that believes in Me, the works that I do, he also shall do; and greater than these shall he do. Because I go to the Father, and whatsoever you shall ask the Father in My Name that I will do that the Father may be glorified in the Son. If you ask Me anything in My Name that I will do.

(John 14:12-14)

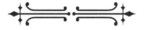

Closing Prayer

I will bless the Lord Who has given me understanding, moreover my reins have corrected me even till night. I set the Lord always in my sight, for He is at my right hand that I be not moved. Therefore my heart has been glad, and my tongue has rejoiced, moreover my flesh also shall rest in hope. Because Thou will not leave my soul in Hell nor wilt Thou give Thy holy one to see corruption. Thou hast made known to me the ways of life, Thou shall fill me with joy with Thy countenance; at Thy right hand are delights even to the end.

(Psalm 15: 7-11)

For Further Reflection
A Living Communion of Saints

+ Imagine the Communion of Saints surrounding you. Which saints do you see? Which of your relatives and loved ones who have died stand out in glory among them? Let your whole body and inner spirit feel their prayers and love warm you and draw you near to them. Peacefully bask in their penetrating love and concern for you.

+ Reflect on an event in your own life which you consider to be a type of genuine miracle; pray in your own words or re-tell the story to others.

+ Pray about your own personal mission on this earth. Like Saints Gabriel, Therese, and Blessed Elizabeth of the Trinity, do you also think about the good you can do on a greater scale from your position in Heaven? With these three saints, imagine the broader and entire picture of your existence in and before God and with and for others.

+ Look around today at all the little, usually unnoticed miracles in your life—a baby's cry, the tree outside your home, a phone call from a friend, your health, the paycheck you receive, the full grocery bags, etc., etc. Give some time at the end of the day to write down your thoughts on these simple gifts and to acknowledge God's providential care for you.

+ Ask Saint Gabriel to intercede on your behalf so that some hurting or broken area of your life will be receptive to God's healing touch.

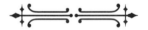

Chapter Seventeen

Becoming Most holy

Saint Gabriel Possenti leads us into church so that we may join him in worship at the Altar of the One Lord. He calls us also to create other holy spaces in our lives where we can retreat in prayerful union with God. The Sanctuary at Gran Sasso is also a powerful image that reminds us that we ourselves must become sacred temples of God's Presence and Light for the world.

Opening Prayer
O God, You have blessed our world with the Sanctuary of Saint Gabriel of the Sorrowful Virgin; in that sacred space, You refresh Your pilgrim people with Your sacraments and an outpouring of the gifts of prayer, healing, reconciliation, and the renewal of Baptismal consecration. Assist us to be men and women of prayerful union with You; empower us to implement the inspirations You give us, becoming the sacred sign of Your love to all we meet. Amen.

The Passionist Community officially returned to their Retreat in 1894 and became the proper guardians of Gabriel's tomb. On May 14, 1905, Gabriel was declared "Venerable"—"heroic" in all the virtues. On May 31, 1908, Pope Saint Pius X beatified Gabriel. The majestic Sanctuary of Saint Gabriel of the Sorrowful Virgin was first started in 1914, attached to the old monastery and enlarging the original church where Saint Gabriel was buried. It was consecrated on February 22, 1920. Venerable Norbert of Saint Mary had once seen this basilica-shrine in a vision shortly before Saint Gabriel died in 1862. Father Norbert was given the grace to see, just for a moment, the great spiritual glory to come through his spiritual son.

On May 13 of the same year, Pope Benedict XV canonized Gabriel Possenti and Margaret Mary Alocoque. In 1921, the Pope honored the sanctuary with the title of Minor-Basilica. Gabriel's sacred bones had been earlier removed from the temporary crypt of 1892 and placed within a bronze sarcophagus, sculptured and hand-painted in the image of the saint and in a position of peaceful repose. The image itself was made in proportions matching the measurements of the full skeletal remains. The image can be opened up in order to maintain the sacred remains, or to retrieve relics, as needed by Passionist officials. Within a glass coffer under the Blessed Sacrament altar, it is clothed in the Passionist habit; the hands hold the very picture Saint Gabriel meditated upon at his death. The pilgrim approaches this special reliquary–which seems to exude Gabriel's spirit–in an oratory to the right side of the basilica.

Stone angels surround the dome of the semi-circular chapel, each holding a particular virtue practiced by Saint Gabriel. Suspended from

the ceiling beneath each angelic figure are deep red-colored glass vigil lamps. In the summer months, when the majority of pilgrims come to the mountain shrine, the reliquary is transferred to a chapel in the modern sanctuary which is adjacent to the old basilica. The new building's cornerstone was laid in 1971; its structure is very contemporary in its lines, and the highest level's roof has an architectural sense of uplifting wings–perhaps to signify Gabriel's soaring spirit and the spiritual quest of the pilgrims. It is a purposefully expansive place for worship, built to accommodate the enormous crowds of people who could no longer fit comfortably in the basilica.

The Italian government also constructed a highway that cuts through the mountains from Rome to the Gran Sasso to meet the traveling demands of the pilgrims. In June 1985, Pope John Paul II knelt in this new house of the Lord before the relics of Saint Gabriel. It was the International Year of Youth; before thousands of youth, the Pontiff preached about the opportunity that was theirs to be modern disciples for Jesus Christ.

In 1988, celebrations were held at the sanctuary marking the 150th anniversary of Gabriel's birth. A fine artist has drawn a contemporary portrait of Gabriel: the background to the left shows Assisi's Basilica of Saint Francis–representing Gabriel's city of birth and his first patron and namesake given to him on his Baptismal day. On Gabriel's right is pictured the Minor Basilica of St. Gabriel in Isola where he died as "Confrater Gabriel;" this latter place of prayer and pilgrimage is the crowning result of Gabriel's surrender to his Baptismal consecration to Christ and the mission God called him to do. Gabriel has not abandoned the mission but continues to call the young and old to Jesus and his Mother's companionship. At times, school children come on special outings and visit the tomb. They have a special Mass and picnic on the grounds. They come away with a sense of pure joy having learned about Gabriel as a spiritual friend and a valuable role model.

The shrine is also popular with young adults and teenagers. They spend the night under the stars in tents, and at dawn they usually join together in song and prayer–experiencing a new Christian solidarity. Buses regularly come with singles, couples, parents, the elderly, and the sick; they seek refreshment of spirit and pray for healing of the illnesses in their lives. The sanctuary is like a fountain in the Church that satiates thirsty spirits. Its great cross looms up as a beacon to all. It is as if Saint Gabriel were holding it aloft saying, "This is the One who was pierced for love of us–He is the *center* of our lives! Follow Him! Come aside and rest awhile in prayer. Seek the Father's Will in your life. Listen to His Word in your hearts. Say **yes** to your personal mission."

The carillon of bells calls the pilgrims to prayer and worship at the Eucharistic altar. They also ring out the Angelus of Mary, the prayer that retells the wonder of the Incarnation. The mountain peaks, covered in snow–even in August–raise the eyes of all to ponder the wonder of God's creation and lift up thoughts to the final ascent in and to Christ. The thrilling view of the amphitheater of mountains is like God's protecting arms wrapping themselves about the town of Isola! The pilgrim's heart sings in return: *For You are my strength and my refuge; and for Your Name's sake You will lead me and nourish me.* (Psalm 30:4)

Consideration
Behold, I stand at the gate and knock.
If any man shall hear My voice and open to Me the door,
I will come in to him, and will sup with him, and he with Me.

(Apoc.3:20)

Pause for Reflection
All you that thirst, come to the water! You who have no money, make
haste, buy, and eat; Come, buy wine and milk without money and without
any price! Why spend your money for what is not bread; you labor for that
which does not satisfy you?

Hearken diligently to Me and eat that which is good, and your soul
shall be delighted in fatness. Incline your ear and come to Me: Hear and
your soul shall live, and I will make an everlasting covenant with you, The
faithful mercies of David. Behold I have given him for a witness to the
people, for a leader and a master to the Gentiles. Behold, you shall call a
nation which you knew not; and the nations that knew not you shall run to
you, because of the Lord your God, and for the Holy One of Israel, for He
has glorified you.

(Isaias 55:1-5)

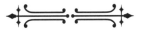

As beautiful as our temples and shrines are, and as magnificent as
God's own natural, outdoor sanctuaries–both compelling us to enter the divine realities–it is essential for true happiness that these precious gifts incite
us to look further within ourselves, permitting our very beings to become
living houses of the Holy Ghost. Through the power of the resurrection,
our daily lives of prayer, charity, and peace will **become holy spaces** for
others to find God within us. People will take their needed rest before our
presence and feel refreshed and soothed by our services of love. They shall
see Christ alive in us. Importantly, too, we ourselves can stop living life
as a mere **reaction** to events and people all around us, and instead, begin
acting out of the Presence of God enthroned within us. This is not the same
as a "higher power" within us which some confuse today with their own
supernatural force. God is our only Higher Power! Thus, our vision and
purpose in life is clearer, solidly fixed in Christ. Unencumbered by other
lesser lights, false gods, and passing fancies, we freely follow and give the

Light. This is the One Lord, undivided Unity of Love, totally other than us who has chosen to abide within us and through us, one with us. We share in this Presence and power and are empowered by God to extend it.

The Word of God

Wherefore, laying aside all malice, and all guile, and dissimulations, and envies, and all detractions, as newborn babes, desire the rational milk without guile, that thereby you may grow unto salvation: if so be you have tasted that the Lord is sweet. Unto Whom coming as to a living stone, rejected indeed by men, but chosen and made honorable by God: be you also as living stones built up, a spiritual house, a holy priesthood, to offer up spiritual sacrifices, acceptable to God by Jesus Christ. Wherefore it is said in the Scripture: Behold, I lay in Sion a chief cornerstone, elect, precious. And he that shall believe in Him shall not be confounded.

(I Peter 2:1-6)

Closing Prayers
Longing For God's House

How lovely are Thy tabernacles, O Lord of Hosts! My soul longs and faints for the courts of the Lord. My heart and my flesh have rejoiced in the living God. For the sparrow has found herself a house, and the turtle a nest where she may lay her young ones: Thy altars, O Lord of Hosts, my King and my God. Blessed are they who dwell in Thy house, O Lord: they shall praise Thee forever and ever. Blessed the man whose help is from Thee: in his heart he has disposed to ascend by steps in the vale of tears, in the place which he has set...For the lawgiver shall give a blessing, they shall go from virtue to virtue: the God of gods shall be seen in Sion...For better is one day in Thy courts among thousands.

AT THE CROSS WITH MARY

I have chosen to be an abject in the house of my God, rather than to dwell in the tabernacles of sinners. For God loves mercy and truth: the Lord will give grace and glory. He will not deprive of good things them that walk in innocence: O Lord of Hosts, blessed is the man that trusts in Thee.

(Psalm 83)

Prayer to the Father in Honor of Saint Gabriel

Father, all-powerful and ever-living God, we do always and everywhere to give You thanks and to praise You for Your gifts as we contemplate Your saints in glory. We praise You for the wonders of Your love in raising up Saint Gabriel to be such an example of holiness in Your Church.

His heart was on fire with love for the Blessed Virgin Mary in her compassion for Your Son. He grew in devotion to the Mother of Sorrows standing at the foot of the Cross and sharing in the Passion of Your Son.

He learned to give himself to you, Father, in heartfelt love. In our unity with him, we seek his fellowship and place our trust in his prayer for us as we look forward in hope to the city that lasts forever.

(Preface, Mass of Gabriel of the Sorrowful Virgin,
Passionist Sacramentary)

Saint Gabriel's Prayer to Mary for a Happy Death

O Mother of Sorrows, by the anguish and love with which you did stand by the Cross of Jesus, stand by me in my last agony. To your maternal heart, I commend the last three hours of my life. Offer these hours to the Eternal Father in union with the agony of our dear Lord, in atonement for my sins. Offer to the Eternal Father the Most Precious Blood of Jesus Christ mingled with your tears on Calvary so that I may obtain the grace of receiving Holy Communion with the most perfect love and contrition before my death, so that I may breathe forth my soul in the presence of Jesus. Dearest Mother of Sorrows, when the moment of my death has come, present me to Jesus as your child.

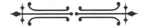

For Further Reflection
As God's Living Sanctuaries

+ Recalling Gabriel's birth in Assisi, consider the call of Saint Francis

from the crucifix of San Damiano: "Francis, rebuild My Church which is falling into ruin." How does Saint Gabriel's call from the Marian icon in Spoleto relate to Francis' mission? How do both their calls to holiness and mission relate to your own?

+ Visit your favorite cathedral, chapel, roadside shrine, or country church. Reflect on what makes this place so special to you. Take in all its appealing details. How does God particularly touch you here with His presence? Sit back and "let go" in the aura and sacredness of this space and time.

+ After receiving Holy Communion, meditate on Mary's *fiat* to the Angel Gabriel and how she became the new Ark of the Covenant! Relate this striking truth to your self as you make your peaceful thanksgiving in the Eucharistic Lord. How does this Reality dramatically change your everyday life and interactions in the world?

+ Make a prayer corner in your home or room and set up an icon, cross, or meaningful image of devotion; or, build a shrine in your garden. Go there often and *pray to your Father in secret*. (Matt. 6:6) Rest in God.

+ Think about your own life when God seemed to shine through you for another person's benefit. How did that person experience the Divine Light in you? What exactly happened? Give peaceful thanks to God and humbly relish and rejoice in the Lord's active love within.

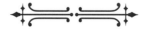

The hidden Face

Author's Notes on
Saint Gabriel's Iconography

Searching for a portrait of Saint Gabriel Possenti I was confronted with a definite obstacle as there were no official portraits ever found in his family belongings and Passionist records. This is a very strange fact, considering that Gabriel was a family favorite, known for his appearance, popularity, and gallant behavior during his collegiate days. The much-circulated old painted-over tintype, discovered in a Passionist Retreat, of a gaunt and sickly-looking Passionist youth, has been regarded by many to be Gabriel's likeness, but it has never been verified. Father Norbert, Gabriel's closest and trustworthy friend and hagiographer, never mentioned such an existing picture; in fact Norbert lamented that there were no actual representations of Gabriel to be seen. Because of this, Norbert had a likeness made of Gabriel from his own description and those who knew him. Norbert was never happy with the resulting rendition.

One other attempt, with Gabriel looking down on the picture of Our Lady of Sorrows was made from a modeling session with Gabriel's niece who was said to have similar features—thus explaining the slightly effeminate rendition and subsequent "too-sweet" iconography of Gabriel. We have to use our own imagination to see those "similar features" of his niece in a sports-minded and virile young uncle. At Gabriel's beatification, Father Norbert beheld the latest picture painted for the great event; he was somewhat pleased, but commented; "…on the whole, it is not him" (Camillus, *Saint Gabriel, Passionist*, pp. 257-8). The British Passionist, Father Wilson, when interviewing Saint Gabriel's brother, Michael Possenti, in 1930, was told that there were oddly no family pictures of any kind for their beloved sibling, Gabriel. Michael showed Father Wilson a recently taken photograph of a masculine and handsome youth, a relative of Saint Gabriel. He felt this photo truly resembled his brother—much more than the portrait modeled on the female relative. He generously gave the photo to Father Wilson who admired it. This picture, sadly, has never been made public and has now been lost.

At the same time, we would be misled to think of Gabriel as some strapping caricature of a "he-man"; he never was anything like that at all. In fact, he was somewhat known for unstable physical health—prone to bronchial and throat infections. Besides, his masculinity was not one-dimensional, but was well integrated with the attractive softness of his genuine warmth of personality, constant polite manners, sensitivity toward the needs of others, and the freedom to express his feelings well and to show affection and devotion. He was truly akin to the world-popular Saint Therese, the Little Flower of Lisieux; she also exhibited great strength of will, spiritual ambition and character blended with a gentle childlikeness. Both saints have been subjected to certain saccharine religious art and statuary of the Victorian and early 20th century periods. Unlike Therese, however, Gabriel never had the benefit of the camera in his monastery cloister. While we are able to study the wonderful spirituality of Therese in her photographed face taken by her own siblings in the monastery, Gabriel's actual face remains in the shadows.

In this particular consideration, Gabriel appears to be like the distorted Face of Jesus, the Man of Sorrows described in Isaias: *No beauty in Him or comeliness; and we have seen Him, and there was no sightliness that we should be desirous of Him.* (53:2-4). I think that Gabriel, so closely associated with the abused and rejected Christ of the Passion, would rejoice in this analogy. After all, it was in the monastery that he struggled to overcome his intense vanity and former attachment to worldly glamour.

And yet, for us who love him, we want to find him more clearly in our thoughts and hearts. We want to see him. And so we search. We might look and catch a more realistic glimpse of him in his wholeness by a study of both his parents' noble and sensitive faces in their formal portrait, or through the dark good looks of his much loved brother, Paul, who also died young, or in the searching eyes of his solicitous brother, Michael. We are fortunate that Gabriel was consistently described by his peers; they saw him as handsome and dashing, winning in his personality and possessing a flashing smile with sparkling black eyes. Norbert "paints" an even more marvelous reality for us: "The light of his interior graces shone out so in the boy's face that he was a marvel of spiritual beauty."

Amazingly, the Gabriel evasive of portraits and photography has been obviously raised up by God to stand out as a powerful sign of sanctity worthy of imitation and veneration. Gabriel's true portrait is a spiritual one, a living legacy of love that has captured the popular imagination and is drawn on the canvases of human hearts. Providentially, Gabriel's face emerges again and again in new ways to warm our hearts and satisfy our need to see him, to know him; in looking into his face, we seem to hear his predominant missionary desire—that we come to Gospel life in Christ and Mary.

In spite of "the hidden face" of the historical Gabriel, compounded by the remote area where he was buried at a time of war, confusion, and subsequent abandonment by the Passionists of the monastic property, Gabriel emerged from obscurity and the dark shadows. His story was told; his memory was held sacred by many. Miracles came from his tomb like a passionate love piercing beyond the boundaries of the grave. His spiritual portrait became etched in the heart of a people and a nation. God has glorified him in Heaven and in our midst. Therefore, the "hidden face" is somehow revealed through the power of the Crucified and Risen Jesus! Gabriel is like the fabled phoenix, a youth lifted up from anonymity, soaring like an eagle, or growing as a fruitful vine in our Church. Passionist Father Zecca insightfully writes that the hidden Gabriel is like one "whose young life is broken off in the midst of a turbulent winter of change and conscience, who returns to us, in deep silence, like a fruitful garden" (*Uno Come Tanti*, p.26). It is my wish that you and I come to know and see Gabriel's true face and spirit more clearly—that we find the same Christian joy that he did in that deep silence of contemplation and in that mystical garden of both prayerful searching and service to others.

A Time for Thanks

I extend my deepest thanks to the Slaves of the Immaculate Heart of Mary for taking this project of re-publication into their hands for the sake of spreading the Gospel message of Jesus Crucified and the love and Motherhood of Mary which Christ entrusted to us from the Altar of the Cross on Good Friday. Special thanks for the loving work and efforts extended in this edition by Sisters Katherine Maria, Mary Elizabeth, Marie-Bernard, and Christopher Margaret. I want to thank Brother Thomas Augustine who gave his blessing and permission to this work.

I also remember all the priests, religious and laity that I thanked in my first edition. You each remain in my heart. Since then both my mentor, Dean Joseph Maguire of Holy Cross College, and my friend, Brother Gabriel Possenti Rivet, OSB, have gone to their eternal reward. I remember you both with deepest love and ask your blessing on this edition that it may go forth to do the mission work of Saint Gabriel. I continue to depend upon and thank the sisterly prayers and support of all the cloistered Augustinian Nuns of the Monastery of Saint Lucy in Rome and the cloistered Sisters Adorers of the Precious Blood.

Finally, I thank you, the reader of this book—and ask Saint Gabriel of the Sorrowful Virgin to place his Passionist mantle about you to protect you, his Passion Seal over your heart so you will experience his true brotherhood in the Precious Blood of the Lord, and finally that his black sandaled feet will walk beside your path on the sacred way to Heaven with Jesus and Mary all the way and in all ways—steadfastly united within the ancient Faith and Tradition passed down to us from the holy Apostles.

John Joseph D. Schweska

December 8, 2008
Solemnity of the Immaculate Conception
(Closing of the Lourdes 150th Jubilee Year)